The
Dorset
Village Book

THE VILLAGES OF BRITAIN SERIES

Other counties in this series include

The Dorset Village Book

HARRY ASHLEY

with illustrations by John Baker

COUNTRYSIDE BOOKS

NEWBURY

First Published 1984
© Harry Ashley 1984
Revised and Reprinted 1985, 1987, 1989, 1992
All rights reserved. No reproduction
permitted without the
prior permission of the publishers:
Countryside Books
3 Catherine Road, Newbury, Berkshire

ISBN 0 905392 35 3

Cover photograph of Kingston
taken by the author

Produced through MRM Associates Ltd.,
Reading, Berks

Printed in Great Britain by
J. W. Arrowsmith Ltd., Bristol

Acknowledgements

My thanks go to Peter Tate, Deputy Editor of the *Evening Echo,* Bournemouth, a Welshman with an unexpected knowledge of Dorset, and Di Pestell who deciphered my scrawl and typed the manuscript, correcting a few spelling mistakes without comment. I am grateful to John Baker, a young artist who gave me the rare pleasure of having my words illustrated.

Finally, my thanks to Nicholas Battle of Countryside Books for giving me the opportunity to write my own book on 'Dorset Dear'.

Dedication

To Mark, who came along for the ride and ate all the sandwiches.

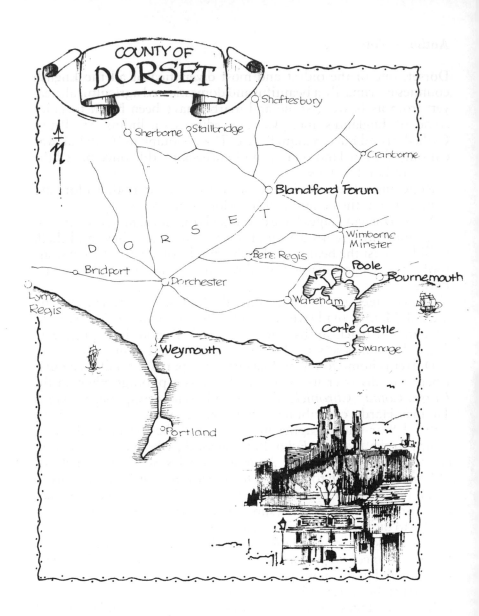

COUNTY OF **DORSET**

Shaftesbury

Sherborne Stalbridge

Cranborne

Blandford Forum

D O R S E T

Wimborne Minster

Bere Regis

Bridport

Poole

Dorchester

Bournemouth

Lyme Regis

Wareham

Corfe Castle

Weymouth

Swanage

Portland

Author's Note

Dorset, one of the oldest and most diversified of all the English counties is primarily a beautiful and domesticated agricultural area, yet, from its bowels, stone and marble have been hewn to grace some of England's most famous edifices, including St. Paul's Cathedral and Buckingham Palace. The Cenotaph in Whitehall was cut out of a Portland quarry, and Purbeck marble once paved the streets of London Town.

Rope manufactured in the west has served both sailor and hangman, but the hemp fields have long since gone.

Many Dorset villages have developed from local material, and little communities centred around coast, downland valleys and chalk hillsides boast the beauty of thatch, and the distinctive heavy stone roofs with sagging gabled windows are prominent in the coastal Purbecks.

The cottages are no longer only the homes of those who live by the soil. Many provide weekend relaxation for workers in town and city, and the blacksmiths' and wheelwrights' shops have given way to gaudy garages serving the needs of tractor and transport.

Dorset is home to me and has been my patch for half a century. I began to discover its beauty in 1936 as a photographer on the *Dorset County Chronicle,* the old traditional newspaper to which Thomas Hardy contributed, after serving in the War as an RAF Official War Photographer in Europe and the Far East, chose to return to the *Evening Echo,* Bournemouth, where a succession of editors, Bill Park, Rodney Andrew, Douglas Sims and Mr.W.M. Hill encouraged me to present Dorset Dear in words and pictures.

It is not a history book; leading historians have provided volumes on those lines. Neither is it a simple guide to the county ... I leave the reader to discover these villages as I have done.

This book is a view of Dorset by a Dorset man; it includes a little history, mixed with folklore, and many personal adventures encountered in my news-gathering.

What is the secret of Dorset's charm?

Dorset cottages are not as picturesque as the black and white half timbered dwellings of the Midlands, and not grouped to the advantage of artist or photographer. Neither can the county boast mountains or poetry inspiring lakes; but this place of untidy villages has one great asset. It is humble and the people are very friendly. They

7

go about their business of rearing cattle and producing the sheep that are famous all over the world, and enjoy the seclusion of their village life.

The cottages wear untidy thick thatch, like tattered tea cosies on stained teapots, and many, 'balding' in old age, are covered with slate or tile. But the spirit of the village and its communities remains. In all my journey, the people I met were kindly, and informative.

Descending narrow lanes, eerie and overgrown, I renewed my acquaintance with places I had not seen for nearly half a century. Not that time really matters. In some of the west villages that saw King Charles II's mad flight to freedom, I was ever expecting to see a troop of Cavaliers or Roundheads come galloping around a corner – so little have the places changed.

Hardy and Barnes have stamped their personalities on the Dorset scene so vividly that I feel oppressed at the places and villages in which Hardy's unhappy characters enacted their strange love affairs. Yet I feel refreshed and free in the Stour valley, with its lovable untidy river winding through the Blackmore Vale to the sea.

This is Barnes country, and he wrote only of the beautiful things in life and, like him, I find great peace along the clote-cluttered river banks within the sound of one of the many mills.

In the east and south of the county popular resorts and picture postcard villages take most of the limelight, but if I have persuaded you to look a little further afield and journey into lesser known Dorset, then I have completed my task successfully.

In the seven years since this book was first published there has been little change in the beautiful county. Only in the east at Ferndown and West Moors has there been any great rise in population where estates service the growing populations of Poole and Bournemouth. It is expected that Dorset will become one of the fastest growing counties and both Poole and Bournemouth now have populations of about 150,000. The far west is practically untouched but Prince Charles' new town is planned on the outskirts of Dorchester.

H W Ashley
March 1992

Abbotsbury 🌿

Whatever time of day visitors ride into Abbotsbury it seems asleep. Even in high summer the ancient yellow-stone cottages neatly tarted up in more colourful hues than they would have worn in the days when they were built, keep their doors closed and cause those who discover this beautiful place to whisper as if they were on holy ground.

This very old village settled amongst the hills behind the great Chesil Bank, which holds the Channel seas in their worst tempers, is known all over the world for its swannery. This bird sanctuary is 600 years old and nestles in the lagoon behind the Chesil Bank. The swans once provided dinners for the monks.

Nine centuries ago, Orca, senechal to Canute, built an Abbey here. Peopled by monks coming from Cerne it dominated the village for over 500 years, and when the Abbey was destroyed during the Dissolution of the Monasteries the great barn remained intact and stands today with the grace of a cathedral, 276 feet long with a doorway more befitting a palace. Little else of the Abbey remains except a portion which forms a gateway to the old vicarage and odd stones which have become built into local dwellings.

Small waterbirds play amongst the lilies on a peaceful pond within the Abbey boundaries, yet once the peace of this Dorset wool-producing centre was disturbed by the crack of gunfire as Cavaliers sniped at Roundheads from the church tower during the Civil Wars, and the oak pulpit still bears the holes from shots fired by Cromwell's men. A bloody battle for the Abbey House ended with its destruction when the magazine blew up.

High above the village on a hill which commands views of the Dorset countryside and the English Channel is St Catherines, a small chapel in the simplest architecture of the Perpendicular period and built completely of stone. This seaman's chapel has withstood 400 years of westerly gales and was a landmark for mariners sailing up the Channel. Now the hilltop is a favourite afternoon stroll for villagers who climb the giant steps formed by early cultivation systems.

Abbotsbury became noisy again in more modern warfare. Off its shores Spitfire pilots fired their machine-guns onto the ranges and the Skip bomb which Barnes Wallis invented to breach the German

ABBOTSBURY   JOHN BAKER

dams was perfected along the coast as Lancaster bombers swept in low, rehearsing for the famous incident.

Once Abbotsbury was reached by a single track railway which chugged through the valley from Upwey under Ridgeway Hill, and the engine was housed in a little brick shed. A line reminiscent of television's Ivor the Engine, but Beeching's axe ended that era.

Those coming direct to Abbotsbury may wonder about the Chesil beach. Legend has it that this mighty bank of pebbles, stretching from Abbotsbury to Portland eleven miles away was washed up in a single night. The facts tell us that it is a million years old and comprises chalk, flint and rocks from distant places. It stands on Kimmeridge clay and when the gales blow and bare the clay, Roman and medieval coins, rings, seals, and gold and silver bars have been found. This was loot from centuries of shipwrecks, for Deadmans Bay, as the Channel waters here are called has claimed countless victims.

The Botanical Gardens and an Iron Age fort called Abbotsbury Castle are worth visiting.

10

Affpuddle 🌿
(with Briantspuddle)

Affpuddle recalls the Saxon Aeffa. It is a sleepy village with its church standing on the river bank and bordered by heath, part of Thomas Hardy's Great Heath.

The church has an early English chancel and Norman font but the pews and pulpit are exquisite. They were carved in 1548 by the then vicar Thomas Lyllington, a monk from Cerne Abbas who came to Affpuddle when Henry VIII dissolved the monasteries. He despised his old companions so much that he carved them into the pulpit, half monk and half fool.

Briantspuddle nearby along a rural road is another of the river Piddle's villages. The cottages are thatched very neatly and they convey a feeling of peaceful idleness, what city dwellers would define as 'real country'. It takes its name from Brian de Turberville, Lord of the Manor in the time of Edward III, and the men of the First World War are remembered on a tall sculptured cross designed by Eric Gill.

Almer 🌿

The Saxons named the village we know as Almer (Aelmere - the eel lake), but this water in which men have caught eels since Palaeozoic days is now almost insignificant.

When I called, the church of St. Mary was locked and in these days of vandalism we know the reason for that. It stands near a magnificent old farmhouse and in its churchyard there is the stump of a preaching cross 1400 years old.

Two novelties make Almer memorable to the visitor. A seven-mile long brick wall, about 8 feet high, links the noble arched entrances to Charborough Park and at the western end of the village, standing back from the main road, is the World's End Inn.

When I first called at this thatched hostelry many years ago, it lived up to its name. A bleak alehouse where you were only welcome if the landlord liked you. Today it is a much bigger building with well lit cosy lounges and a stable bar serving delicious food. It is the sort of end of the world we would all like to come to.

Alton Pancras 🕊

Set among the hills in the very heart of Dorset is this small village with its lovely name.

Originally it was called Awultune, a Saxon name meaning 'the village at the source of a river', the river in question being the Piddle.

At the time when the English bowmen overcame French armour at the Battle of Agincourt, the village was known as Aulton Pancras, by adding the dedication of its church to the Saxon name. The original church was almost in a state of collapse when it was completely rebuilt in the late 19th century. All that is left of the old church is the 15th century tower and part of the Norman archway. The roof is of the scissor beam construction, supported by corbels of the popular Ham stone, and the floor tiles were made at Poole Potteries.

The church of St. Pancras shares its name with a famous and busy London Station but how many people know about the sad and short life of this saint?

He was a young noble born in Phrygia and orphaned when he was ten years old. His uncle Dionysius took him to Rome to be educated. He became converted to the Christian faith, and at the age of 14, after the death of his uncle, Pancras was brought before the Emperor Diocletian and told he must either renounce his faith or be thrown to the wild beasts.

Bravely the lad informed the Emperor that he dare not deny his Saviour, who would give him the strength to die if he must.

Diocletian was naturally enraged and ordered soldiers there and then to slay the boy with a sword, which on reflection was probably a quicker death. So Pancras became a Saint and this little church in the heart of peaceful Dorset is dedicated to him.

The church has an interesting organ, which began its life in a fairground, but has been added to in an effort to give it a sweeter tone.

A manor house has a five bay East front with an unusual colour scheme of purple brick with red and yellow dressing.

12

Ansty ✳

On the chalk uplands of Dorset, lived on by Romans, Britons, and earlier men who worked in bronze, are many picturesque villages, including Higher and Lower Ansty, Pleck, the alternative name for Little Ansty, and Ansty Cross. Relics of these bygone inhabitations are still found, but it was a publicity-minded vicar who in the 1970s brought fame to Ansty.

The Rev. David Pennal revived the ancient ceremony of Randy Day, after 65 years. It is the day when youths of the village armed with 3ft long randy poles, made of bamboo and decorated with streamers, chase the village girls. Those they touched were supposed to give in to their amorous advances. Whether in the more permissive 20th century the ceremony got out of hand I do not know but it has not been repeated since.

Over Xmas that same year, 1976, the vicar organised a world record Housebrick Push. Thirty three year old, 18 stone Terry Mears pushed 298 housebricks, weighing 12 cwt 71 lbs., a distance of 27 feet, in a standard wheelbarrow, and locals combining with 121 villagers from Hilton, Melcombe Bingham and Cheselbourne sat on each others knees in an unsupported circle.

Incidentally Ansty comes from the Saxon and was first recorded as Anstigan from the word Anstiga, which meant a narrow path on a hill. Pleck is an obsolete word for a plot of land.

Arne ✳

Arne was once described as a 'lonely, lovely place where the Great Heath comes down to the wide blue waters of Poole harbour. Here is the peace of loneliness, for there is no voice save that of seabirds and wind'. That was before the Army decided to use it as a battle training-ground during the last war and the few houses were practically demolished.

When peace returned the village suffered further shame because modern smugglers unloaded their contraband on Arne's quiet shore.

Slowly Arne was rebuilt and the tourist can walk the lovely road across the heath from Wareham, splendid in all seasons; cloaked in

13

russet for winter and ablaze with colour when summer heath blooms. In fact the walk is the best part of visiting Arne, because there is little else but its small 13th century church built by the monks. The village name comes from the Saxon, Aern, which means 'a house'.

The church of St Nicholas is built on the side of a hill and is well buttressed. The body and chancel are under one roof. Of architectural interest are the heads of the triplet windows which are hewn out of one single stone and the view from the altar windows is one of the loveliest in Dorset. To complete the church's charm, it is lit by candlelight.

If you are interested in bird watching there is more. Arne has a Nature Reserve, twelve hundred acres of it. A nature trail is laid out for visitors during the summer months, but parts of the Reserve can only be visited by permission from the RSPB Warden at Wareham, because amongst the many fine and rare species that can be seen is that rarest of birds, the Dartford Warbler, a tiny bird with dark grey plumage above and russet beneath.

This long-tailed bird is talked about in various parts of Dorset, but I have never met anyone who has actually seen one.

Ashmore

This village, right on the borders with Wiltshire, is the highest in Dorset and stands 700 feet above sea level. In its centre is an attractive large pond which is rarely dry, with ducks and waterfowl in evidence. It is clearly a Romano-British site and owes its existence to the pond. The Manor Farm is an attractive building, parts of which are medieval, with one addition built early in the nineteenth century as a Wesleyan meeting room. It remains a quiet and secluded enclave in rural Dorset, and has a Roman road from Badbury Rings to Bath passing through part of the parish.

When winter wraps the Dorset countryside in snow, the village, off the high road from Blandford to Shaftesbury will quickly feature amongst the places completely cut off by the drifts, but visit on a sunny spring morning, when all that grows green is new, you will be aware of an unbelievable feeling of peace.

You are alone with the song of the birds and the resident ducks. Artists come to paint the lovely stone buildings reflected in the still water, and if you are lucky a string of racehorses will briefly mirror themselves as they pass, but it is the bird song that thrills most. A symphony of cooing doves and pigeons form a bass to the canorous calls of the blackbirds and smaller birds and the occasional dissonant quack of a duck.

On a day in May, I was lucky to see ducklings so small that I feared for their safety as they strutted into the water, but soon they overcame their surprise at the fussy water ringlets which rippled the pond, and were racing into deep water.

An elegant War Memorial names five men who perished in the 1914 war and a young pupil pilot of the South African Air Force who found his corner of a foreign field in a village far from the violence of war, in 1941.

Ashmore also has religious peace and on the notice board of the church of St Nicholas I read that a service was being held with the Methodists sharing.

In the church, rebuilt and dedicated in 1874 though its chancel arch, re-set, dates from the 13th century, there is a strange memorial. A plan of 350 graves looks like the lay out of berths in a yachting marina. A key gives all the names and the framed plan is in memory of Brig. James Montague Carew Hoblyn who died in 1905. Another proud exhibit is the broken tombstone of John Mullen who died in 1652. It was retrieved from the old church.

Just outside the village on the High Down there were breathtaking views of the Cranborne Chase. The downhill slopes of Stubhampton Bottom across the Roman road looked primitive, the undergrowth speckled with bluebells. The road to Farnham was a patchwork of various greens. Grass, young crops and here and there great squares of brilliant yellow, the oil seed rape. In other parts of the book you will read of my dislike of the Chase, because its history recalls killings and awful happenings connected with man from prehistoric times to the Civil Wars. Also, I seem destined only to visit in drab winter days and usually on unpleasant assignments.

Here on this May Day I stopped the car on a grass sward where bluebells in clusters carpeted around the tree roots. Below me, beyond the remains of camps and burial mounds was Farnham, and across the Dorset border, Tollard Royal. No landscape could have been more beautiful.

Athelhampton

As the motorist speeds into Puddletown on his way to Dorchester, he is apt to miss one of the most interesting homes in England, hiding behind the trees. Athelhampton Hall is mainly 15th century, with a Great Hall, an oriel window, and unique timbered roof. A new wing was built at the beginning of the 16th century.

The Martin family, the first being Martin of Tours who came over with William the Norman, and his successors lived here for 400 years. The sad end came in 1595 when Nicholas Martin was buried in Puddletown church. He had no heir to succeed him. The saddened man had this written on this tomb, 'Nicholas ye first, Martyn ye last. Goodnight Nicholas'. It is now undecipherable.

Wandering in the acres of landscaped gardens of the beautiful home we can sympathise with Nicholas as he watched his four daughters at play on the lawns, and longing for a son to inherit the Hall.

Earlier residents included the Knights de Londres and de Pydeles, who were there in the time of Richard II.

Batcombe

Even the official notes issued by the church of St. Mary Magadalen at Batcombe tell the strange story of 'Conjurer Minterne', a squire in the 17th century who is supposed to have leapt his horse from the steep hillside over the church, knocking off one of the pinnacles on the tower which, they say, was replaced in 1906.

Perhaps it is a ruse to entice visitors to come down the precipitous Batcombe Hill, a narrow lane descending rather in the manner of a helter-skelter ride, to see the church. There is little else but a few cottages and a well-thatched farmhouse.

Although the roof of the church tower is visible from the hillside, believe me the leap was impossible. Even showjumper Harvey Smith, in his most belligerent mood, would not attempt it.

The place has another legend. On the summit of the hill is a mystic stone called the Cross-in-Hand. Although an unpicturesque monument, there are those who believe they can see the shape of a hand grasping a bowl at its top. Those of such mind will probably tell you that it was the place of a terrible murder, or where a miracle was performed.

16

Ascending the hill, I found the appearance of a 12 foot crucifix on a lonely corner of the wooded slopes far more eerie. It marks the entrance to the Friary of St Francis, where Brothers test their vocation and wayfarers are cared for.

In 1973 the bells were stolen from lonely Batcombe church but were recovered at Ringwood a few days later. This almost forgotten village has known more important days. In 1864, over 180 people lived here and, much earlier, a cottage called 'Minternes Folly' was used as a poor people's home. The 'Poor Lot', from which the poor were allowed to cut wood for fuel, is situated in Chips Lane, on the West Hill, and the practice is still allowed.

Other lanes with interesting and amusing names include Drywater Lane, Greathead Lane and Wriggle River Lane.

Like many other Dorset villages, too remote to attract commuters the population has dropped. In 1864, there were 184 villagers, but in 1972 that figure had dropped to 69, of which 19 were over 60 years of age.

Beaminster

If you saunter into Beaminster at lunchtime and wander through the narrow streets that converge on to the Square, there is a feeling that this little place resembling a village, yet actually a town, stood still at the turn of the century and has been enjoying a prolonged siesta for the last eighty years. Only the television aerials, ugly overhead cables and cars which park neatly in the Square, indicate that this is the 1980s.

The sombre buildings with nineteenth century dates carved beneath their eaves have not suffered greatly from the modern tendency to clothe old walls in bright, colourful washes.

The 16th century church tower, magnificent and dominating, is adorned with sculptures of the Madonna, the Crucifixion and the Resurrection. Built in yellow stone, it is one of the finest in the county.

In more violent days, it is recorded that men were hanged from this tower during the reign of James II, but it was more peaceful when Dorset poet, William Barnes descended the green slopes which surround Beaminster and inspired him to write these lines.

'Sweet Be'mi'ster, that bist abound
By green an' woody hills all round,
Wi' hedges, reachen up between
A thousan' vields o' zummer green,
Where elems' lofty heads to drow
Their sheades vor hay-meakers below,
An' wilde hedge-flow'rs do charm the souls
O' maidens in their evenin strolls.'

Beaminster has suffered from the ravages of three great fires in 1644, 1684 and, a century later in 1781.

It is not the fact that this place was the centre of the making of the famous, now extinct Blue Vinny Dorset cheese, which Treves described as the cheese without which no Dorset man is really happy, that made little Beaminster internationally famous.

Thomas Hine, Beaminster born, gave his name to Cognac Hine, recognised as the 'connoisseurs' cognac'.

Thomas, born in 1775, left seventeen years later to seek his fortune in France. Although it was at the time of the Revolution, he found employment in a brandy business at Jarnac on the Charente River. He was no fool and married the daughter of the house, became a partner and eventually reached ownership. He suffered persecution because he was British and refused to relinquish his nationality.

Shortly after the Napoleonic Wars, he gave his name to the company. He died at the age of forty seven years in 1822. Incidentally, his son became the first Briton to be elected Mayor of a French town.

Around Beaminster are the notable houses of Mapperton, Melplash and Parnham, the latter being the most interesting.

Its long history is worth recording because this beautiful west Dorset house which has seen foul murder and has had many owners, today is famous as the home of the Makepeace school for craftsmen.

The earliest record of Parnham is during the reign of Richard I when it was owned by Stephen de Parnham. The first Parnham House was built about 1400 by the Gerard family and it passed into the hands of the Strode family in the reign of Henry VI when Richard Strode married Elizabeth Gerard, and it remained in that family for three hundred years.

18

The estate flourished because the Strodes had the knack of marrying rich wives and not only did they benefit from the large dowries, but each Strode married twice! In 1522, Sir Robert Strode married the daughter of Sir John Hody, Henry VIII's Lord Chief Baron of the Exchequer and her considerable fortune helped him rebuild Parnham.

The long reign of the Strodes was not always a happy one and the family was divided during the Civil Wars. Lady Ann Strode was beheaded in the Great Hall of Parnham by one of Cromwell's soldiers.

In 1776, Parnham descended through the female line to the Oglanders of Nunwell, on the Isle of Wight. William Oglander commissioned the fashionable architect, John Nash, to restore and enlarge the house in 1810. Amongst his plans for re-modelling the house was the installation of Strawberry Hill Gothic windows in the dining room and on the exterior he added buttresses and battlements.

1896 saw the arrival of Vincent Robinson who, having purchased the house, filled it with Rennaissance furniture and works of art, which he had collected from all over Europe.

Early in the twentieth century the house was bought by Hans Sauer who was intent on restoring the Tudor interior.

After Sauer's death, Parnham was owned for a while by a family associated with a war nearer our time. William Rhodes-Moorhouse was the first pilot to win the Victoria Cross posthumously in the First World War, and he lies buried in a private grave with his son, born at Parnham, who was shot down in the Battle of Britain.

In the 1920s, it became a country club often visited by the Prince of Wales and it was requisitioned in the last war and used first as an army hospital and later as an H.Q. for the American army. Some of the planning of the assault on the beaches of France took place at Parnham.

The latest phase in the Parnham saga began in 1976 when John Makepeace, the furniture designer, bought it from the Mental Health Association which had owned it since 1954.

The empty and sad building was an embarrassment to the local authorities after its long and turbulent history, but Makepeace has given it a new vitality. He moved his cabinet making business from Oxfordshire and began his business at Parnham. The furniture made by John and his apprentices is of the twentieth century, each piece designed and built for individual clients. The timbers, naturally seasoned at Parnham, are mainly the fine British hardwoods, oak, ash, sycamore, cherry, yew and elm, but sometimes exotic woods are used. The young members of the team undertake a five year apprenticeship.

A non-profit making Educational Charitable Trust provides funds to run the school for young craftsmen, opened in 1977 to help those whose ambitions were frustrated by lack of a training establishment. The trust has an impressive list of patrons including Sir Peter Hall, Sir Roy Strong and Yehudi Menuhin.

Visitors to this ancient house have the added pleasure of watching the young community at work and being in the lively atmosphere of the new Parnham. Exhibitions of contemporary artists' work, including pottery, silversmithing and sculpture are held each month and amongst items of interest around the house is the four poster bed in the Strode Room, made in the workshops from a single yew tree.

There are fourteen acres of gardens surrounding the house and the River Brit wanders along the western boundary.

Parnham is an ideal setting for those who love to sit and turn their minds back over the centuries, re-live the past and visualise the residents in colourful costumes flitting across the yew-lined terraces. Parnham with a famous past still plans for an exciting future.

Belchalwell

The interest stirred by this strange name is soon dampened, because – to the Saxons over ten centuries ago – it simply meant the hill by the cold stream. The Normans built the little battlemented church on a mound, but it seems deserted by the village and only a few cottages remain.

The lane to the church is narrow and overgrown, but R.K. Palmer, in *What's In A Name*, pens some amusing observations on the 'ceade-well' (cold stream), part of the village name.

'Did the warriors complain that the cold water gave them stomach ache, or was it the womenfolk who grumbled on wash day?' he asks.

It is thought that once it was two villages, later joined, because in 1286 the place was known as Belle and Chaldwell.

20

Bere Regis

A modern highway has been built to by-pass Bere Regis and this ancient village is now a quiet precinct, free for the visitor to explore in peace.

The infamous King John had a palace of sorts here and about the year 1000 AD, Queen Elfrida, never having recovered from her dastardly deed at Corfe Castle, (see Corfe), died in a nunnery.

On the credit side, Bere was the home of Simon de Montfort, founder of our Parliament, but pride of place historically must go to the Turbervilles, who came in the reign of Henry VIII and remained for centuries. Without a doubt they are the more famous because Thomas Hardy chose them as the basis for his D'Urberville family and such is the power of Hardy's writing that we have almost become convinced that Tess, a novelist's fancy, really lived, and may believe she actually came across the heath to Wool Manor. The D'Urbervilles have upstaged the Turbervilles.

The church is a splendid 15th century edifice with an arcade built by the Normans. The lovely pillars have capitals richly carved, but of all the wonders of this church the roof takes pride of place. It is crudely carved and gaudily painted. Twelve remarkable figures look down on the congregation. The twelve Apostles are garbed in colourful 15th century dress and are unique.

Today Bere seems wearied by its past but a few years ago was briefly awakened by a whirlwind which swept down the main street damaging many of the old cottages.

Bincombe

This sad little hamlet nestles close to the great Ridgeway Hill like a kitten cuddling close to its sleeping mother. Bincombe Barrow, high above, overlooks Weymouth Bay and Portland beyond. In Napoleonic times it was the site of a military camp, but fighting men looked out from this point a thousand years before.

In the 1930s, when the British Home Fleet comprising several capital ships, aircraft carriers, cruisers, destroyers and submarines, assembled in Weymouth Bay – it was a vantage point to watch exciting searchlight displays. White beams weaving in the darkened sky, silhouetting the shadowed ships as they produced the set patterns of light. A spectacle that will never be seen again.

In the days when we observed the silence for wartime dead at the eleventh hour of the eleventh day of the eleventh month, and the whole country came to a halt, I watched an old bearded ploughman stop his team of horses between the furrows, and lift a watch from his waistcoat. Removing his flat cap, he bowed his head. A lonely vigil, probably remembering a brother or perhaps a son. The Ridgeway has witnessed many facets of war.

Bincombe had all its livestock wiped out by an outbreak of foot and mouth disease in the mid-1930s but the village had its finest hour in a Christmas Day broadcast, during those pre-television days when on the 25th December everyone gathered around wireless sets, to be conducted on a world tour on the holy day. Shortly before the King's speech, Ralph Wightman – Dorset's famous dialect broadcaster – against a background of the church organ music, described the simple village scene as farmer and farmhands and their families, in Sunday best, filed into the little village church to remember the birth of a Saviour. Suddenly the whole world was aware of little Bincombe, beside a hill, in Dorset.

Bourton 🌿

It is the last village in Dorest but the historians ignore this place, divided by the main A303 road bearing heavy westbound traffic. Some claim Silton as the most northerly village, but the honour goes to little-known Bourton, situated right on the border near the Three Shires Stone, where Dorset meets Wiltshire and Somerset.

Feeling neglected, the villagers have told the story of life in Bourton, 1984 style, on a video film. They hired the equipment and recorded village scenes and made interviews with residents, farmers and children ... preserving for all time the way of life and some dialect. The film includes a social evening with skittles and country dancing.

Bourton has few farms and the largest employer is a plant processing dried milk. Like many other Dorset villages, its is only a few miles from a town, and a large housing estate has grown up on one side of the main road, the mixture of villagers and estate dwellers forming new social problems, brought out in the film.

The BBC made a television feature of the Bourton amateur film makers at work, so it is no longer a forgotten village.

Mere is just over the border and readers must forgive a disciple of the Dorset poet, William Barnes, if I digress for a moment to visit the Wiltshire village where young Barnes, whose name will frequently appear in the Dorset village story, ran a school. In the well preserved and cossetted Tudor Chantry House, beneath the 13th century church with tall elegant, pinnacled tower, William Barnes taught in the years he was trying to impress his future father-in-law that he was a hard working suitor, and not a dreamer.

The lawns, which he once cut, slope down to a lake carpeted with water-lilies just allowing enough water to reflect the church tower.

I know of no place more tranquil and beautiful and natural, and in the little arbour on the lakeside he wrote his best sonnets, including this final memory.

'Sweet Garden! peaceful spot! no more in thee
Shall I e'er while away the sunny hour.
Farewell each blooming shrub and lofty tree;
Farewell the mossy path and nodding flower!
I shall not hear again from yonder bower
The song of birds or humming of the bee,
Nor listen to the waterfall, nor see
The clouds float on beyond the lofty tower.
No more at breezy eve, or dewy morn,
My gliding scythe shall shear thy mossy green;
My busy hands shall never more adorn.
My eyes no more may see, this peaceful scene.
But still, sweet spot, wherever I may be,
My love led soul will wander back to thee.'

Bradford Abbas 🐚

Mention Bradford Abbas and a smile crosses my lips because it is a reminder of the days when I got the taste for what my mother would call 'strong drink'.

She was very much against alcohol having seen my sea-faring grandfather and her mother often the worse for it.

My protestation that as a newspaperman it was part of my duties to visit pubs and meet people were ignored.

'It will shorten your life', she said.

Then on my travels I called one day at the Mitre hotel in Shaftesbury and saw on the wall a calendar portraying five old men who were from Bradford Abbas sitting in a line quaffing pints of ale. Such were their beards that they looked as if they were made up for a film.

Filmed they were; 'The Lads', whose ages totalled 444 years, not only advertised the goodness of the ale, but became famous in the 1930s when a Newsreel Company screened them and they were portrayed nationally.

Sam Ring (92), Thomas Coombs (91), James Higgins (89), George Chainey (89), and Sid Parsons (83) not only became celebrities but went to town to see themselves on the big screen.

All had taken an active part in the life of the village. Tom Coombs had taken his rope in the church bell-ringing team and Sam Ring proudly carried the big banner of the Friendly Society on fete days, but what I am about to recall could not have happened in these days of sexual equality.

Whilst 'The Lads' were lapping up all the glory, it was kept very quiet that the village also had five 'Old Girls' who could offer a fair challenge to the menfolk.

Mrs Edward Parsons (91), Mrs Mary Jane Munckton (87), Mrs E. Patch (84), Mrs Gladys Good, (84), and Mrs F. Wills (82) made up a total of 427 years.

True to the attitude of their sex at that time, they never begrudged 'The Lads' their glory. Probably not wanting to give their ages away.

The story, however, did nothing to change my mother's views on the evils of strong drink.

One of the satellites of Sherborne, cosily constructed out of the gold Liassic limestone which is now, unfortunately, beginning to show its age.

Some modern building has used the same soft stone but though the material can be matched, the artistry cannot. A 15th-century church is remarkable for good carved bench-ends, particularly near the chancel entrance.

The Rose and Crown Inn, built in the 15th century, possibly as a monks' rest-house and afterwards used as a malt-house, has a grand stone fireplace with good panelling above it.

The ancient church is claimed to be one of the finest in the county, with a medieval tower ninety feet high, it looks like a miniature cathedral. The canopy over the Jacobean pulpit was removed to make a table.

Bradford Peverell

John Hutchins, most famous of all Dorset historians, was born in the village of Bradford Peverell, near Dorchester, in the shadow of Poundbury Hill, in 1698.

The east window of the church, one of the few in Dorset with a spire, has some ancient windows. The east window has fragments of 13th and 14th century glass from New College, Oxford.

Dr. Howley, once a rector here, rose to become Archbishop of Canterbury and it was he who crowned Queen Victoria.

Branksome

Between the boundaries of industrial Poole and the healthful parklands of Bournemouth lies Branksome, a complex area of wealthy estates and working class homes. It is the centre of Borough jealousies and snobbery, because the vast village of Branksome which at one time had its boundaries well inland and almost into Bournemouth Square has two separate communities divided by a railway line. There is still a strong village community spirit within each.

Branksome has one side called the Park and the other literally on the other side of the tracks, an area mainly of terraced residences built around the Gas Works. The latter does have its beauty spots, amongst them Coy Pond, where swans and geese entertain the visitors. The gardens around the Bourne were developed with ornamental bridges in 1850, nearly twenty years before Bournemouth set out the Pleasure Gardens.

Early prints of Branksome show sheep grazing on the banks of the Bourne. Bransome Park is the area which stretched through the lovely woodland to the Chines, now developed for the pleasure of visitors at Branksome and Branksome Dene.

The Park estate belonged to C. W. Packe, M.P. for Prestwold, Leicestershire. In 1852 he built a plain stone Tudor house to a design by the Scots Romantic, Robert Burn. An earlier single towered building was on the site.

The drive to the house is now the Branksome Avenue, and until recent years the Lodge at the Westbourne entrance to the Park was used as an Estate Agent's office, but a new gyratory traffic scheme and the erection of large office blocks completely changed the area.

It was long known as County Gates (where Dorset and Hampshire met before the county boundary changes). If you look carefully, a small fragment of the lodge wall has escaped demolition.

Later Packe's home became the Branksome Towers Hotel, a famous hotel of quality where Royalty stayed, and it was run by one family until the 1960s.

The avenue became a broad boulevard flanked by mansions, amongst them Cerne Abbas, described as a Wagnerian fantasy and built in 1890 in red brick Gothic with a high chateau roofed tower, but both hotel and house have been demolished during the last decade with other proud Victorian properties and the Avenue is now lined with blocks of modern flats as well as the site of the Branksome Towers Hotel.

Gone also are the magnificent rhododendrons which dominated the Avenue, in twenty foot high banks separating the road from the foot-paths. Muggers and molesters loitered to catch the unwary and sadly the magnificent bushes have been cut to waist height. Both the Chines are now hut-lined bathing beaches belonging to Poole Corporation who have developed the sites without spoiling them, but a ghastly murder shortly after the last war caused acres of the Dene to be levelled in the search for clues, when Neville Heath was charged with the murder of Doreen Marshall. The devastated land was utilised as a car park.

In 1893 there was a rustic bridge over the Dene Chine from which the young Winston Churchill fell whilst climbing the woodwork and his life was feared for. How different might our modern history have been if young Churchill had died in a Dorset Chine.

It is the amusing situations which reflect the jealousies between Poole and Bournemouth.

Bournemouth, with health giving pine trees and an orchestra frequently broadcasting over international networks, became a world famous resort and the 'city fathers' of Poole developed an inferiority complex, claiming that Poole was far more important than young Bournemouth.

26

'We have ancient charters making us important, we even sent four ships to the Seige of Calais', one respected mayor once told me, forgetting that most citizens of today cared little about such historical facts and were interested only in the lowering of rates. Further anger was caused when many Branksome residents started naming Bournemouth in their correspondence. The last straw was the Branksome Towers Hotel's insistence in their advertising that they were in Bournemouth.

The publicity officer at Poole was under constant pressure to keep writing to newspaper editors informing them that Branksome was in Poole.

Poole had no need to feel inferior because she has become the fastest expanding Borough in the country and her population will soon overtake that of Bournemouth. The Bournemouth Symphony Orchestra now has its home in Poole.

This town pride in ancient charters (the first was granted in 1248 by William de Longespee) is nurtured by the Society of Poole Men. They regularly beat the land and sea bounds of the Borough. County Gates at Westbourne was one of their boundary points. They read their charter loudly so that the Bournemouth people on the other side of the road would hear it.

When the authorities tore up the road at County Gates, making it unrecognisable with a large roundabout which served as an island home for an insurance company, the Society of Poole Men became perplexed, because they could not find the exact spot on which the boundary stone stood. It was an anti-climax when they found they had to carry out their ceremony in the centre of the island car park belonging to the new office block.

In 1969 a reminder that Branksome was once an Urban District was given when a skin diver lifted a large stone from the harbour bed. It bore the letters B.U.D. and it was first thought that the stone was a pet's tombstone.

However, it was soon verified that it was an old boundary stone of the Branksome Urban District, which became part of Poole in 1905.

Another amusing story concerns the boundary with Bournemouth. Before the last war, the aged Duke of Connaught spent an annual holiday at the Branksome Towers Hotel. Each day he descended to the sea front with his aide for a constitutional walk along the promenade.

In those days the publicity committee of Bournemouth Council were generous to Press photographers, giving handsome bonuses for pictures mentioning Bournemouth which appeared in the national newspapers. So the cameramen used to wait on the Bournemouth side of the boundary for the Duke and could then truthfully say that he was holiday making in Bournemouth.

Broadmayne

It is a sign of my misspent youth that I remember Broadmayne because I often detoured to find myself there at lunchtime where they served bread and cheese and home made pickled onions for sixpence, at the Black Dog Hotel. My expense allowance would just cover that plus a pint of Dorset ale. It is the bread I remember most, half a cottage loaf, so hot that the butter melted as it spread.

The village straggles along a mile or two of the Dorchester to Wareham road till you reach Warmwell Cross.

In the village the notorious highwayman Bill Watch stabled his horse when he was raiding the coaches on the Weymouth to London run. The barn he used is now converted into a dwelling.

For a village which produced quality bricks from locally dug clay for over one hundred years it is out of keeping to find the old Manor House, thought to be 13th century, covered in 'bricks' only half an inch thick. On closer inspection it can be seen that they are actually tiles stuck on in the late 19th century as protection.

Behind the house is a granary supported on stone staddles, the peculiar mushroom-shaped foundations which prevent the entry of rats.

Mentioned in the Domesday Book, the village was once called Maine Martel, the Martel family being Lords of the Manor in the 12th and 13th centuries.

Broadstone

Broadstone scarcely existed two hundred years ago. Heathlanders living in scattered cottages cut turf for fuel here, but there are relics of those who had lived or passed this way before. An arrowhead, dated to 1500 B.C. was discovered on the slopes of Springdale

Road, and a 17th century stirrup from the restless days of the Civil Wars was found in Clarendon Road area, but historians give no clue as to how it may have got lost there.

Today Broadstone is an elegant suburb of Bournemouth and Poole. The slopes overlooking Poole Harbour and the Purbeck Hills encouraged the wealthy to build lovely properties there long before the last war, and the vast building estates which have grown up since 1946 have maintained Broadstone as a quality area. A large shopping centre lines the main road and like many London suburbs built around villages, the older part of the village lives in harmony with the new.

So named because of the broad stones laid as a means of fording the Blackwater stream, close to Brookdale Farm, Broadstone was first recorded as a village in 1765. The Roman road from Hamworthy was close to the present village and was the boundary of Canford Magna parish, but now it is the border between Broadstone and Corfe Mullen.

In its short history, Broadstone has witnessed the arrival and departure of the railway. Although the line came through in 1847, the station there was not opened until 1872. This facility lasted about one hundred years until Beeching axed the line and where the railway passed under a bridge at the village centre, a complex road roundabout has been constructed.

The last train out of Broadstone will be remembered by train spotting enthusiasts who gathered on that historic Sunday morning to see the train depart, loaded with other rail buffs.

As cameras clicked, the guard posed on the platform, trying to obey all the instructions of the photographers when, waving his flag at their command, the engine driver thought it was time to leave, and the train pulled out. The memory those photographers will retain was of the portly guard chasing along the sleepers to regain his charge.

The Golf Club has attracted many famous personalities over the years, including a former Bishop of London who was not popular with some of the caddies. In addition to carrying the clubs, Dr. Winnington Ingram required his caddy to walk behind him and help push *him* up the steeper slopes of the course.

Broadstone has known a host of famous and unusual residents. Most famous was Alfred Russell Wallace, the biologist, who with Charles Darwin, was co-discoverer of the theory of evolution. He did not come to Broadstone until he was seventy eight years of age and in his lifetime, had explored the Amazon and Malay Peninsula. He liked unusual homes, and his house at Old Orchard has been described as dark and inconvenient. This man who was known for his scientific thinking and his views on spiritualism, socialism and vegetarianism is buried at Broadstone and his grave marked by a fossilised tree from South America.

As a boy, the actor Richard Todd resided in the village and the Dutch playright, Jan Fabricus, lived at Caesars Camp, a house on Broadstone Heights. Although little known in this country, he was one of Holland's most famous authors. A pet bird always sat on his writing desk.

Broadstone was also the family home of the Hibberds. Stuart Hibberd was the B.B.C's first Chief Announcer in the days when radio was the dominating media. His was the cultured voice of Britain and he will be remembered for his announcement when King George V was dying. 'The King's life is moving swiftly to a close'.

It is thought that by the year 2,000, Broadstone will have forty thousand inhabitants. That could be an underestimate.

Broadwindsor

There is a touch of comic opera in the flight from Worcester by the future King CharlesII.Hewas searched for in the household of Sir Hugh Wyndham at Pilsdon (see also Pilsdon), where pursuers thought he might be disguised as a woman, when actually he was at Broadwindsor dressed in the garb of a lady's servant. In the little village inn, there took place an episode of history that is more like a scene from a 'Carry-on' film farce.

Soon after the royal party arrived and went to an upstairs room, searching Parliamentary troops turned up and demanded accommodation, so the prince's party could not leave without passing the pursuers in the bar. Then, by sheer luck, a rumpus was raised in the village over a dispute about a baby born to one of the camp followers. The authorities were afraid that the child would be left in their care as a pauper. Such was the performance and argument that the soldiers returned to the inn exhausted and went straight to bed, leaving the way clear for the royal party to quietly steal away.

The Castle Inn was burned down in 1856 but a cottage on the site carries a plaque commemorating his stay.

The village remembers with pride the Rev. Thomas Fuller who made his congregations roar with laughter during his sermons, a rare event in the 1600s . Because of his humorous writings he was known as 'quaint old Tom Fuller'.

After the Monmouth Rebellion the son of John Pinney, minister of Broadwindsor was sentenced to be deported for his part in the fighting. Because of the family's position, they were landowners and prominent lacemakers, the son Azariah was given preferential treatment and transported to the West Indies as a free emigrant. Once there he extended the family business acting as his father's agent in the lacemaking business and other ventures. He made a fortune for himself whilst his fellows on the boat *The Happy Return*, which sailed out of Poole spent their lives in poverty and degradation.

Brownsea

The visitor pays his toll and can now wander all over the romantic Brownsea Island, and in summer watch Shakespeare's plays in an open air theatre, but it has lost the magic and mystery that surrounded it in the days when it was privately owned.

Some of the owners were eccentrics, others famous, but none more interesting than recluse Mrs Bonham Christie who kept the island as a bird sanctuary, and callers were decidedly not welcome. In fact during the 1930s she employed 'a blonde and powerful female Scandinavian PT instructor' (I quote the National Trust Guide) to throw visitors off the island.

Mrs Christie's reclusion was a challenge and in 1947 I joined the Poole Pirates at a Bounds Beating ceremony and coaxed the Pirate Chief, ships chandler Steve Colombos to land on the island and confront her. Steve, a diminutive figure, wore Wellington boots which reached up to his knees and under his large floppy hat rather resembled Paddington Bear.

The creaking door of the island's castle opened slowly and the little white-haired old lady appeared and asked our business.

'M-Mam', stuttered Steve, a little overawed, 'my friend wants to take your photee'. She smiled, came out on to the quay and posed with the Pirates.

Brownsea, now under the control of the National Trust is one of the last outposts of the red squirrel and the sound of peacocks re-echoes through the woods.

Although Baden-Powell held his first Boy Scout camp on the north end of Brownsea in 1907, it was a hermit monk who over 1400 years ago did the first good turns, and lit a beacon at night to guide sailors into the vast harbour.

In its long history, Brownsea, also known as Branksea and Bruno's Island has exported daffodils, and in 1853 a Col. Waugh went bankrupt mining china clay which proved worthless. It was the luckless Colonel who spent £10,000 on the beautiful church. Henry VIII built a square blockhouse at Brownsea to protect Poole and amongst its former owners was William Benson, famous for getting Sir Christopher Wren dismissed from his post as Surveyor of Works.

The island shores have witnessed a cavalcade of ships through the ages. The Romans passed in their galleons and today sleek and expensive pleasure yachts moor in the lee of the island, playthings of the members of the more exclusive yachting clubs of Poole.

Buckland Newton

Amongst lush north Dorset meadowland and hills gentle and rounded, lies Buckland Newton – a timeless place which has known Roman and Saxon habitation.

Saxon law was administered by the King and approved by the Witan, Bocland being land given under charter by the King, distinct from folkland occupied by right of common law. As the village grew, it became known as Niweton and Bocland, 'The new town and land held under charter.'

The church with 13th century chancel has a 'rude' carving of a saint above its door. Dug up in the vicarage garden, it could have belonged to a church built there over a thousand years ago, and the figure is possibly St. Thomas.

A pleasant little room with a fireplace above the porch, reached by a winding stair, is thought to have been used by monks who came over from Glastonbury to preach. Because the church is not built exactly east-west a sundial has been placed crookedly on the porch wall.

Those who love the writings of William Barnes will tarry awhile at a tablet in memory of Thomas Barnes, who died eight years after Shakespeare. He was a wealthy ancestor of William, who was born of a more humble farming family, but who made the vale of Blackmore, in which Buckland lies, famous by his poetry. In 1937 Buckland Newton was chosen by the BBC as a typical Dorset village.

Burton Bradstock

Here, Dorset's 'great barrier reef' – Chesil Bank – comes to an end, 15 miles from its start at Portland.

The pebbles here are smaller as a result of their constant bombardment by ocean currents.

The river Bride flows past Burton's one-sided main street but the wanderer should not be held by the view across the water of thatched cottages and the attractive Dove Inn.

The real Bradstock lies in the labyrinth of byways behind – Donkey Lane, Darby lane, and Shadrack to name but a few. There is a touch of London in this home of fishermen. The clock in the 500 year old church came from Christ's Hospital, the home of the famous Bluecoat Boys, when it stood in Newgate Street.

Grove Hill House once produced linens and sailcloth from the three mills in the village.

When Bournemouth smuggler Isaac Gulliver opened up a Western connection, he used the beaches of Burton Bradstock to unload his contraband. He bought a farm at the foot of Eggardon Hill and planted a clump of fir trees on the top of the hill as a landmark for his ships, his farm being a useful centre for the customers in Bath and Bristol.

Canford Cliffs

This elegant little village on a hill-top overlooking Poole Harbour, like Branksome Park, is another wealthy residential area. On its slopes it has a very modern church designed by Lionel Gregory in 1962 to replace a little Mission Church built in 1911.

Nikolaus Pevsner, in his *Buildings of England* described Canford's pride and joy as 'the exact ecclesiastical equivalent of Dunromin and Thisledo'. He disliked its bungaloid appearance.

33

PALM COURT

COMPTON ACRES.   JOHN BAKER

Few locals would agree with him. The simplicity of the interior is a feature, decorated with timber from the old church.

The pride of Canford Cliffs are the beautiful gardens of Compton Acres. Four owners are responsible for the creation and upkeep of this showpiece which delights thousands of visitors each year.

At the end of the First World War, Thomas William Simpson bought the Neo-Tudor Compton Acres Mansion, built in 1914, and conceived the idea of surrounding it with a unique series of independent gardens, planned so that only one garden could be seen at a time.

At the turn of the century, the land had been wild moorland, a wilderness of golden gorse and purple heather, the yellow sandy slopes densely clad in Scots pines. The backcloth to this wild beauty was Poole Harbour, Brownsea Island and the Purbeck range of hills.

On these slopes, Simpson set out his sylvan walks, green lawns, terraces, lily ponds and fountains.

It took several years of intense activity and an expenditure of about £250,000 before the gardens evolved.

Thousands of tons of stone, rocks, and good earth were collected. Rare plants, some tropical and sub-tropical were brought in from all over the world.

In the unique Japanese garden, every plant was brought from the Far East in a specially chartered cargo vessel which also transported the gardeners who laid it out and planted it.

The Second World War took its toll of the gardens and the death of Middleton, the famous head gardener, quickly followed by that of the garden's creator, William Simpson, spelled the end for this former oasis of beauty. The inadequate staff could not recreate and maintain the gardens. The rhododendron banks became impenetrable jungles, and the tall trees merged their branches overhead, blotting out the life giving sun. 'Even the birds deserted', one old gardener told me.

In 1950, Compton Acres was saved. Architect J. S. Beard, who designed many English cinemas during the cinema boom, purchased the property, restored it and re-opened it to the public.

Alternative routes were designed around the gardens so that the infirm could avoid the steps.

It was one of the new owner's pleasures to sit by the side of the fountain in very old gardening clothes and when a happy visitor said "I would like to meet the man who is lucky enough to own all this', he would would beam and reply, 'Well you are talking to him now'.

In 1956 he added a very personal touch to the beautiful gardens. He built a little circular picnic garden, walled in Purbeck stone. It was a memorial to his son Dick, killed whilst flying with the R.A.F. in 1942, and to his two young daughters who were tragic victims of polio.

John Brady bought the gardens in 1964. John and his wife hailed from Devon. The Bradys enjoy sharing their home with the visitors and realise that without their support, it would be impossible to maintain this splendid estate where, in the course of half an hour, the visitor can find himself in distant Japan, or in a Roman garden, beside an Italian lakeside, or in a simple English garden with velvet lawns and flowering shrubs and the old fashioned flowers of the country.

The gardens were sold again in 1985 and Simpson's fine house turned into flats.

Canford Magna

The village of Canford Magna now has complete peace. It has lost its railway and a new main road bypasses the great house, steeped in history and, since 1923, one of our younger public schools. It stands in 260 acres of lush park on the banks of the river Stour. The village has a mixture of thatch and quaint buildings, mostly serving as residences for teaching staff, and the little traditional state school is now used as a village hall.

The imposing Canford School was once the battlemented house of the Guests, and Lord Wimborne had a coach road built with two bridges crossing main roads to enable him to drive straight to Bournemouth Central Station.

The house was erected early in the 19th century around the older building which, in its time, had housed Salisburys, Montagues, Beauforts and Mountjoys. Boys at the School can sit and study under the trees that were probably there when the Black Prince came.

In its long history the romantic thriller story of Ela, Countess of Salisbury and William Longespee, a famous knight, is worth recounting. Ela was a wealthy woman and Richard the Lionheart chose her to wed his stepbrother, William. It was a happy marriage but as Earl of Salisbury and Lord of the Manor of Canford, he was often abroad fighting. A long delay in his return from France led everyone to think he was dead.

Hubert de Burgh, the villain of our story, urged her to marry his nephew but she refused, being sure she would one day see her husband sail into Poole.

Her wish came true and William returned, although ill from privations and exposure at sea. He was not pleased with Hubert and, during a reception at Salisbury Cathedral, they quarrelled and William died. It was rumoured that Hubert had poisoned him but it seems more likely that William died of ill health. Lady Ela retired to a convent but it was her son, William Longespee, who granted Poole its charter in 1248.

Cattistock

The pride of Cattistock was its renowned carillon of 35 bells cast in Louvain, the first in England. Their mellow tones rang out over this large village, with a church more befitting a city. Alas they were destroyed in a fire in the tower in 1939.

The grand church was designed by G.G. Scott, eldest son of famous architect, Sir Gilbert Scott.

The earthworks on Castle Hill defy dating, but King Alfred's grandson, Athelstan, gave land hereabouts to the monks in return for their prayers. Today the Cattistock Hunt, one of the leading packs in the West Country, roam over the same hills.

A feature of the fine church tower used to be an enormous clock face which spanned the whole width of the tower, but it has been replaced with a face of more normal proportions. The nave is not particularly homely but visitors are drawn to an enormous font cover of pyramidical shape which, elaborately carved, reaches almost to the roof.

The Caundles
(Bishops, Purse and Stourton)

The Caundle villages, rich in pastureland, lie in the heart of William Barnes country in the north of Dorset, and his poem, *Bishops Caundle* was written after the victory at Waterloo.

> 'At Peace day, who but we should goo
> To Caundle for an hour or two:
> As gay a day as ever broke
> Above the heads of Caundle vo'k,
> Vor Peace, acome for all, did come
> To them wi' two new friends at hwome.
> Zoo while we kept, wi nimble peace
> The wold dun tow'r avore our feace
> The air at last, begun to come
> Wi' drubbens of a beaten drum;
> An' then we heard the horns loud drouts
> Play of a tuen's upper notes;
> An' then agean a risen chearm
> Vrom tongues of people in a zwarm;
> An' zoo at last, we stood among
> The merry feàces o' the drong.'

It is a long poem with a description of the feast and dancing on the village green to the accompaniment of musicians platformed on a gaily painted farm wagon.

> 'In Caundle, vor a day at least,
> You woudden vind a scowlen feace,
> Or dumpy heart in all the pleace.'

Today it is a dour village with church and churchyard dominating the main street. It feels old especially when you remember that men who saw the hail of arrows at Agincourt probably talked about it in this same street, because the village name goes back to the legend of Arthur, and the Dark Ages. Caundle is a Celtic word, a name given to the chain of hills which look from Dorset toward Somerset. In Domesday Book it is recorded as Candel. In the 13th century it became Caundel Episcopi. The Episcopal owner of the land at the time was the Bishop of Sarum.

Purse Caundle is a village which always seems at peace with itself. At its centre is a 15th century church and a beautiful Manor House. In 1241 the village was called Purscaundel, Purse being the old English word for priest.

One of Purse Caundle's most illustrious sons was one born Peter Mews, whose story would be excellent material for a swashbuckling film. Very briefly, this romantic figure of the Civil Wars was an undergraduate and a soldier of Charles. Always in the thick of battle, he received about 30 wounds. He was taken prisoner, became a fugitive and a royalist agent in Holland. He was a master of diguises and was nearly hanged.

Ordained, he became Bishop of Winchester in 1684, at the age of 66 years. When the Duke of Monmouth started his revolt, he went back to war and, in victory, pleaded for clemency for the misguided rebel. The old Bishop Cavalier died at the great age of 91 years, but does not rest at Purse Caundle – it would probably be too quiet for him.

Hithe Paradise is the name of a field in Stourton Caundle – and very aptly named because this delightful village has a clear stream running past its thatched cottages. This Caundle takes its name from the Stourtons who lived here long ago in a castle long since gone. Only the chapel survived and that does duty as a farm building.

Cerne Abbas

Mention Cerne Abbas and thoughts turn to the very rude giant, carved into the chalk hills, probably before the Romans came.

My late colleague, Pat Palmer, was highly amused when a geographical magazine pronounced him an authority on the giant because he advanced the theory that the large sexual organ of this hideous figure associated with fertility rites, was so enlarged because at some period a restorer has wrongly incorporated the giant's navel with other parts. The carving is 180 feet high with the 7 foot long fingers holding a 120 foot long club.

The villagers are rightly annoyed that the giant is their main fame, because Cerne is a very old and beautiful place, with fine old world streets – a joy to film makers – and was once a famous coach staging post. It seemed destined to become a leading West Country town.

Cerne was disheartened when it lost its proud Benedictine Abbey in 1539, but tried to build up its industry with shoe making and the brewing of fine beers. But, when the railways came and bypassed Cerne, it was literally the end of its progress.

Today Cerne tries to forget the dreadful bloodshed and tragedy of earlier years ... of Margaret of Anjou and her idiot husband, Henry VI, the poor feeble King of England who was destined to be the last of the Lancastrians. Cerne now concentrates on providing a show-piece village for overseas visitors and, in excellent inns and cafes, entertains the people who come to see this example of a fine old world town.

Cerne cherishes the remains of her Abbey, founded in 987 AD. It now consists of a gatehouse and a guesthouse situated behind Abbey House at the end of a truly ancient street in which stands the church. The Abbey's 14th century tithe barn is at the southern end of the village. The mainly 15th century church, with much older chancel, was restored in the 1960s, and the rotting pews replaced with chairs. The bells did not ring for 70 years because the hangers were unsafe but in 1974 the bells were recast and a sixth added to the peal.

A modern memorial in this place of ancient history is a seat in memory of a schoolmaster who with his pupils created the BBC programme, 'The Village'.

Chalbury 🐚

There is a green hill between Horton and Wimborne with an unusual white-walled church clinging to its 330 foot summit. Little else remains of the old village of Chalbury, but a new generation is discovering this lovely place, of which historian Hutchins remarked 'the air is clear and wholesome.'

Apart from the breathtaking view offered from the hilltop, encompassing lush Dorset farmland, Ringwood Church, Cranborne Chase, and, to the south, the Channel with the white-walled Needles predominant. It has been an aid to navigation and a naval communications link.

Once, a great elm tree, so large that it could be seen from the sea, was a daylight mark for mariners coming up Channel and, until the 1950s a little telegraph cottage with spiral staircase – one of the chain of semaphore communications stations between Plymouth and Whitehall – stood in the corner of the reservoir. To no avail, author Pat Palmer of the *Evening Echo*, Bournemouth, tried to save this Napoleonic relic. Without ceremony, it just disappeared.

The lovely church, the oldest parts of which are 13th century, is squat, simple, with the smallest of square towers, and has high sided family box pews, with doors, which enabled the elders to snooze during sermons and the young to indulge in a little sly courting.

Chaldon Herring

Kinkiness has become accepted in the permissive 80s, with androgynous personalities in colourful garb, hair styles which range from the mohican to macaw, and a complete freedom of sexual expression; so it is relieving to note that earlier Dorset residents also had some queer ideas.

On the summit of a hill near the almost forgotton village of Chaldon Herring, which lies between Winfrith and coastal Ringstead, are 5 burial mounds, in a line, known as the Five Marys. In death, the Bronze Age men and women were given a burial place with a view across the Frome valley to the Great Heath of Winfrith, but when one of these graves was opened they found skeletons of a man and woman sitting together with the antlers of a stag on their shoulders. The Norman church, rebuilt in the 15th century, has a rare Saxon font discovered in a farmyard and brought to the church in this century.

Churchman and craftsman Canon Gildea made the beautiful pulpit and lectern with his own hands.

The three famous Powys brothers, who were all novelists, knew and loved this village well. On the hill between the village and the sea there is a memorial stone to Llewellyn Powys which bears the inscription

LLEWELLYN POWYS
13th Aug 1884
2nd Dec 1939

The Living. The Living. He shall praise Thee.

Charminster ✿

The magnificent Wolfeton House, for generations the seat of the Trenchards, almost commands motorists heading into Charminster to halt – even if only to admire the circular towers with conical roofs which support the gatehouse. Built by Sir Thomas Trenchard in 1505, it was remodelled in the time of James I.

Because it was such a stately residence, it was to this house that the Archduke Philip of Austria and his wife Joanne were brought after being shipwrecked at Weymouth in 1506. So aware was Joanne of her noble birth, that she donned her finest clothes so that if she was washed ashore dead, she would have been given a funeral fit for a Spanish princess.

However, she survived and the people of Weymouth brought her to Sir Thomas Trenchard at Wolfeton. Sir Thomas, not speaking Spanish, sent for his kinsman, John Russell, who lived at Long Bredy, to come and act as interpreter. As told in the entry on Swyre, John accompanied the party to King Henry VII, became a favourite at Court and founded the House of Bedford.

The church is 12th century with Norman chancel arch and nave arcades supported in typical rounded Norman pillars. Sir Thomas Trenchard added the tower in the 15th century.

The river Cerne flows beneath the church and during heavy rain in the 1890s, a cartoon appeared in the church magazine depicting the congregation sitting knee-deep in water with umbrellas opened as the vicar preached from the pulpit, also under an umbrella.

Charminster is proud of its identity and dislikes being linked with Dorchester. In 1960 a Roman villa with mosaic pavement was unearthed in the village. Some of the residents, appalled by modern vandalism, have suggested bringing back the office of a Beadle to help the police.

Charmouth ✿

Jane Austen found this village a nice place for 'sitting in unwearied contemplation', but that was when the predecessor of the A35 echoed only with the hard melodies of coach wheels and horses' hooves.

Now not even a wealth of thatch and Regency bow-fronts can disguise the close proximity of a busy trunk road.

The village is situated in one of the few gaps in the hills which break into the cliffs overlooking Lyme Bay.

The oldest pub is the Queen's Armes. When Catherine of Aragon stayed there soon after her arrival in England in 1501, it was still a house built for an abbot of Forde. By 1651, when the fugitive Prince Charles was looking locally for a fast boat to France, it had shed all inhibitions and become a hostelry.

The conversation piece most likely to have caught Jane Austen's copious ear in 1811 – though there is no proof that it did – was the discovery of a strange fossilised creature in the cliff-face by 12-year-old Mary Anning. Later minds identified it as the famous ichthyosaurus which now abides in the London Natural History Museum. Fossils are still there for the taking but the possibility of a monumental find in these well-travelled days is remote, but school children still come in official parties and burrow away at the cliff-face to the dismay of conservationists.

Cheddington

Cheddington, high up in the chalk hills of West Dorset is the source of two rivers, the Axe and the Parret. It is remarkable for its exciting views. The National Trust gave 16 acres of their land as a memorial to the 43rd (Wessex) Division of the Dorsetshire Rgt. On a bluff stands an impressive monument – a replica of the memorial on Hill 112 at Caen in Normandy, which is forever associated with the 43rd.

At the north end of the village is a famous cutting called Winyard's Gap, and from this point the road twists downhill to cross the border into Somerset.

The Winyards Gap Inn, tucked beneath an ancient earthwork, has seen all manner of traffic over the centuries, but history does not tell us how many inns have stood on the site. Armies have certainly marched by, as have countless flocks of sheep and herds of cattle on their way to market. King Charles I led his troops through the Gap in 1644 with kettle-drums beating out a rhythm, and until comparatively recent times colts and fillies trotted past on their way to Dorchester.

The innkeepers often had other activities in the community, and not always legal. There are tales of smuggling (it was not far from Gulliver's western connection). No doubt highwaymen halted

43

many a traveller at this lonely spot. Incidentally, the name Winyard comes from Anglo Saxon Wynheard.

It is a story concerning gypsies, prostitution and a court case which rocked London that brought fame to the Gap. The case involved such personalities as Henry Fielding, author of *Tom Jones* and *Amelia*, who was a man who would fight social evils of all kinds. The inn at Wynyards Gap was part of the alibi of a gypsy called Mary Squires, who with brothel keeper Susannah Wells were the principal defendants.

On New Years Day 1752, eighteen year old Elizabeth Canning, who was in service in London, went missing for a month. She arrived home in a sorry state claiming that Wells and Squires had kept her virtually a prisoner in a house for immoral purposes. She aroused much sympathy and interest in her predicament. Although Fielding stirred up support for this 'poor' girl, John Hill a Quack doctor rallied those who did not believe her story . Gypsy Squires claimed that she was travelling in Dorset and during January was with her family at the Winyards Gap Inn, then called the Three Horseshoes, and at a nearby village inn at South Perrott.

The case was proved and the two women were found guilty. Squires was sentenced to hang but a new champion came to her aid, none other than the Lord Mayor of London Sir Crispin Gascoyne, who just happened to be the Master of the Brewers Company, who went to a great deal of trouble checking Gypsy Squire's pub-crawling story nearly two hundred miles away in rural Dorset.

He not only earned Squires a pardon but the naughty Elizabeth Canning was convicted of perjury and sentenced to transportation to a penal colony for seven years. The branding punishment which had already been carried out on Susannah Wells could not be erased.

Today's visitors come to the Gap to enjoy the majestic views. To the north east are the Mendip Hills and the Hamdon Hills from which the rich golden-coloured Ham stone is hewn to grace many of the lovely Dorset mansions.

Cheselbourne 🌿

The church of Cheselbourne is well worth a visit but beware of the hazardous car ride through a lane scarcely eight feet wide with a three feet drop into the fresh running stream.

44

Why the builders in 1295 set St. Martins on the slopes where they had to level the ground is a mystery, unless they wanted it to be near the Celtic fields which spread across the heart of Dorset to the Piddle valley. There is a tomb dole table near the main door, as well as preaching cross. The records recall that there is a plague pit where hundreds are buried. Brilliant white snowdrops now erase the memory of that horror.

The church tower was built 500 years ago and the worm-eaten timbers removed from the bell loft are stone-hard. The re-hung bells rang out again in 1981.

Amongst the many absorbing features in this simple church, the neat kneelers in royal blue are most impressive. All have individual tapestry designs in bright colours, one depicting young shepherds and a flock of sheep. The kneelers are the work of Cheselbourne women, and not all church members.

There are interesting sundials in the church. One is dated 1631 and another earlier dial is scratched onto the wall.

Chesil Beach

Life without sound would be unbearable. I did not realise its importance until, covering the Barchi earthquake in 1962, I wandered deep into the Sahara Desert. There alone, I experienced a complete silence. It made me shiver. Sounds trigger off memories.

India reminds me of rickshaw bells and the cacophonous mixture of traffic and the calls of street sellers in Calcutta's Chowringhee. Burma recalls tinkling temple bells and the squeal of dry axles on ox cart trains, resembling a modern symphony.

In my childhood I recall being lulled to sleep by the distant 'drub of Deadmans Bay, where bones of thousands are', as storm waves thumped the Portland beach.

This Dorset phenomenon of pebble, which is what its name, Chesil, means, has no equal in the world. It stretches from Portland to Burton Bradstock and although it has an inglorious history, one wonders what the Channel would have made of the coastline without this defensive barrier. It appears frequently in the stories of our coastal villages, but deserves a mention in its own right.

Statistically, its length from Portland to Abbotsbury is 10 miles, but it extends to Burton Bradstock. At Portland it is 40 feet high and

CHESIL BEACH (PORTLAND). JOHN BAKER

600 feet at its base. The pebbles, which gather from many parts of the coast, stand on a foundation of Kimmeridge clay and vary in size, getting smaller towards the west. Fishermen who come ashore in fog can ascertain where they are by the size of the pebbles.

On a summer's day, it looks like a giant yellow snake snoozing at the water's edge. That is when the Channel is in gentle mood, but I know of nothing but evil and tragedy about this awful place.

As a child, I watched terrified as a great steamer, with her propeller thrashing the air, ended her days wallowing against the beach and later was assigned to see the three masted schooner, *Madelaine Tristran,* carrying a cargo of gin, grind herself into the beach.

Rescue has always been difficult because the steep bank runs straight into deep water, and thousands of seamen and soldiers have perished on this beach of death – some sucked back into the awful sea.

There have been evil people ashore who lured ships to their doom with lights, plundering the wrecks and pushing the crews back into the fearsome waters. In 1748, the *Hope of Amsterdam* carrying £50,000 in gold, was wrecked. A crowd gathered like vultures waiting to loot. The shore was a scene of riot and barbarity as they fought in the darkness for the gold. Some strangled others whose pockets already bulged.

Amongst the variety of treasure washed ashore over the centuries, was a great carving portraying the crucifixion of Christ from a wrecked galleon of the Spanish Armada ... and a mermaid!!

What the strange creature was we shall never known but it met its misfortune at Burton Bradstock in 1757.

46

It was 13 feet high or, if you prefer your mermaids lying down, 13 feet long. The famous historian, Hutchins, who relates the finding, gives us a clue as to his body preference. He says 'Her upper or better half had human form while her extremity was that of a fish. The head was partly like that of a man and partly like that of a hog. Her fins resembled hands. She had a masculine jawbone and 48 teeth in both upper and lower jaw'.

Chettle

The north-east of the county, encompassing the Cranborne Chase, has a sinister atmosphere. The whole area is dotted with burial mounds and has a long history of brutal struggles for existence.

For centuries men killed men in this bleak corner of Dorset and, when they were not so engaged, they killed the animals that roamed wild.

Chettle, one of the villages, is built in a wooded hollow, a secluded place. It has two ancient long barrows, dug over 2000 years ago as the final resting place of Neolithic Stone Age farmers. Its seclusion made it a good place to live in times of trouble, and the Chafins set up home here in the 17th century. Thomas Chafin opposed the advance of the Duke of Monmouth and commanded a troop of Dorset Horse at Sedgemoor.

Poor Monmouth must have disliked the Chase as much as I do because he had several traumatic experiences there. Some of Thomas Chafin's letters to his wife, Nan, have been preserved. One passage written in a letter dated July 1685 from London, I find amusing:

'I hope to be home Saturday sennight. The late Duke of Monmouth's head was severed from his body yesterday morning on Tower Hill about 10 in the forenoon. Lord Grey will soone be there too. Blessing to the bratts. So farewell my dearest, deare, Nan.'

Happily 'dearest deare' and Thomas died natural deaths. He in 1691 at 41 and his wife 14 years later. A tablet in Chettle's beautiful church records their deaths but the house next to the church where she brought up 14 children, has been rebuilt in Queen Anne style.

So perhaps the story will not seem strange when I relate that a Chafin came back to live at Chettle in 1914 and, whilst writing a book *Anecdotes of the Cranborne Chase*, was struck by lightning. However, he lived to finish the book.

Chideock

Pronounced 'Chiddick' this village is another casualty of a tussle with the A35 but a village rather more accustomed, from its history, to alarming sounds and the hot breath of mobility.

This was always staunch Roman Catholic country and it was in the main hall of Chideock House (now the Chideock House Hotel, priest's hole and all) that the Chideock Martyrs were tried.

The present R.C. church, dedicated to Our Lady of the Martyrs and St. Ignatius, was built in Romanesque yet highly original style in 1870-72 by the Weld Family, who had succeeded generations of the Catholic Arundell family at the beginning of that century.

Sir Joseph Weld, past lord lieutenant of Dorset, is also acknowledged as one of the leaders of today's Roman Catholic community in the area. (see also Lulworth.)

The village is filled with well-built and well-maintained cob and sandstone cottages, some of them thatched, all of them colourful with gardens which seem so planted as to ensure graphic flowering at any time of the year.

The 'Chideock Gang' in the 18th century, were a select band of smugglers who limited their activities to the coast between Seatown and Charmouth. Their leader, 'The Colonel' cloaks the name of some local gent who obviously had military training. The gang had a magnificent look-out post on the top of the 617 foot High Golden Cap.

Compton Abbas

The year that saw the birth of this village was a year of war for Alfred, but, between nine battles with the Danes, he founded an Abbey at Shaftesbury and made his daughter Abbess. The Abbey was endowed with the rich land around and, at the foot of Melbury Hill, now lies the village we know as Compton Abbas. A place of peace was born in a year of turmoil. The Saxons called it Cumb-Tun (a village in a narrow valley). In the 13th century it became Cumton Abbatisse, a lovely sounding name which, I believe, should have been retained.

The peace Alfred hoped would always be here was shattered in the 1970s when a small airfield was established on the hill above the village. Although only used for light aircraft and the towing of gliders, the villagers started a long battle to prohibit flying, but they did not win their cause until the 1980s and, for the moment, all is at peace again.

There is the stump of an old preaching cross in the churchyard, and a stone mounting block to aid a farmer's wife of long ago to get aloft on her horse, but the ancient church is no more. Only an ivy-covered tower remains and the bells which once rang there are now in the new church.

Compton Valence

The residents of Compton Valence can boast that in the days of the Romans it was the place where Dorchester derived its water supply. Situated in a hollow of the hills it lies close to the Dorchester – Bridport Roman road.

The church is dedicated to St. Thomas and was rebuilt in 1838. The nave was lengthened and a north aisle added, and the reconstructed chancel was given an apse-shaped end wall. The 15th century tower was saved.

Portland and Ham stone were used in the re-building and Bath stone was introduced for the pulpit. The Caen stone altar was later replaced by a wooden Communion table. The Williams family instigated the re-building. The four bells in the tower are dated 1620, but were all re-cast in 1870, and a modern touch, the 19th century clock was electrified in 1979.

Corfe

The murder of a king, and an early attempt to prove women's equality are but two of the strange events in the long history of Corfe.

This now peaceful village of stone, clustered around the hillock which bears its famous castle, has no equal in England. The majority of visitors who come to capture its beauty with camera and canvas have little knowledge of the treachery and bloodshed that is woven into Corfe's history.

CORFE VILLAGE AND CASTLE.   JOHN BAKER

The people who live here tell you so with pride because their village has been named amongst the most beautiful in the land. They keep the cottages, some cloaked in warm-coloured creepers, neat and tidy, but I cannot walk its streets without feeling a cold shiver as I recall the past, to be revived in one of Corfe's splendid inns which are warm and friendly.

The dominant castle standing on its own conical mound, a majestic ruin in a cleft of the Purbeck range, has nothing to guard and it is whimsically suggested that a Norman or Plantagenet castle builder saw the site and thought it a magnificent place to build a castle and lord it over this part of England. Three little streams surround its base to meet and flow into Poole Harbour as Corfe river.

Its history began long before the Normans built a castle. The Romans knew it and in Saxon times a lodge was built on the site to house those who hunted in the Royal Forest of Purbeck. The widowed Queen Elfrida was in residence when her stepson, young King Edward, tired from hunting called for refreshment. She was jealous of Edward, wishing her own son Ethelred to reign. She brought him a cup of wine and as he drank it, plunged a dagger in his back. Some say a servant did the deed, but it matters little because he galloped off and died in the saddle on the way to Wareham. The murdered king was canonised as Edward the Martyr and the Corfe church dedicated to him.

In remorse, the Queen is said to have retired to a nunnery at Bere Regis.

King John starved 22 knights to death within Corfe Castle's walls, and imprisoned Isabel and Margery, daughters of the King of Scotland. John further bloodied Corfe's history by having Peter of Pomfret dragged from there behind a horse to Wareham and there hanged.

Perhaps I have disillusioned those visitors who wander through Corfe's peaceful byways, browsing in the souvenir shops, but there is more. Eventually the castle came into the Bankes family and was prepared for service for the King in the Civil Wars. During one attack, when Sir John Bankes was away, Lady Bankes with her servants and maids beat back 150 Poole seamen by pouring hot ashes over them as they tried to scale the steep banks, but later the castle fell by the treachery of an officer of the garrison. Parliament ordered it to be blown up in 1645.

Quarrymen invade each Shrove Tuesday in happier circumstances. They hold a court where young apprentices are initiated at a ceremony which includes the carrying of a quart of ale into court as veterans try to steal it, and the kicking of a football through the streets to preserve their right of way.

Corfe has had an abundance of characters, like innkeeper Teddy Brown who turned some of the floodlights illuminating the castle onto his hostelry, the Fox, and a veteran who read his evening paper whilst holding a lighted candle long after electricity had arrived in the village.

It is said that one night a very inebriated villager was found by a policeman wandering home long after hours. He explained 'I bin watchin television at Mr Brown's pub'. The policeman retorted 'There has been a power cut since 8 0'clock'. The reveller was undefeated. 'I know', he said, 'but Mr Brown got the gas'.

I once climbed one of Corfe's surrounding hills after a pleasant hour in the Fox, and resting awhile looked down on the castle ruin and tried to visualise it in the days of its greatness. I must have dozed because my reverie was violently disturbed by the crack of gunfire. Corfe still hears the noise of war from the nearby Lulworth ranges.

Corfe Mullen

A main road separates the ancient part of the Stourside village of Corfe Mullen from its blanketing residential area on the hill above it. The church of St. Hubert stands at a crossroads keeping an eye on both sides of what must be one of England's largest villages.

On the hilltop are the school, supermarket and sports centre servicing large and varied estates which stretch all the way to Broadstone, a dormitory for those working in Poole and Bournemouth.

Old Corfe Mullen, down by the sleepy Stour, shows all the signs that it is in the hands of people who care and maintains its character in spite of constant traffic speeding past the doors.

The old mill, mentioned in Domesday Book, churns its rebuilt wheel in what is now the centre of a tea room. A glass case softening the clack of the noisy wheel and splash of the Stour. Next door, the Coventry Arms still maintains flag stones in one of its bars, but the lounge offers a cosy welcome, with warm lighting around the bar.

The church had its first rector in 1162, and the little 300 year old Manor House, across the road, hides its beauty behind trees. Obviously it is only part of the original building, a fact given away by the massive six chimneys.

Historian Hutchins tells us that it was the home of the Phelips family, who left money to Corfe Mullen partly for the better maintenance of the curate, and partly to provide bread and cheese every Sunday, and beef at Christmas, for ten poor children.

Corscombe

Corscombe, north of Beaminster was the home of another of the county's odd characters. Thomas Hollis, the rich squire had simple tastes. His family had always been benefactors of John Harvard's University since 1690, and in the 18th century he carried on the good work. It is said that hardly a ship sailed out of London without gifts from the Hollis family for Harvard University, and Thomas's gifts included priceless books.

When his home was on fire this man, described as a 'True Whig', quietly walked out clutching only his portrait of John Milton.

He rejected alcohol, milk, sugar and butter and had a fear of dying of a lingering illness. He need not have worried because in 1774 he dropped dead in a field whilst issuing instructions to farm hands. He had no religious beliefs and they carried out his request to be buried in his own fields ten feet deep and the land ploughed over so that no trace of him was left.

Corscombe lies in lovely wooded country with its main street climbing up the chalk hillside. It is one of the most peaceful parts of Dorset, so it is sad to associate it with the bloody deeds of 1685 after the Battle of Sedgemoor.

Robert Fawn of Corscombe who was with Monmouth was hanged with twelve others, their bodies dismembered, then boiled in pitch and publicly exhibited.

The infamous Bloody Assize at Dorchester resulted in 74 executions, 175 transportations and 9 floggings.

George Penne who owned Weston Manor and Oak Farm at Corscombe was given 100 prisoners as part payment for helping to put down the rebellion. He sold most of them as indentured servants to planters in America and West Indies. However, in 1890 as Brigadier General he assisted William of Orange at the Battle of the Boyne to defeat James Stuart.

It is a chapter in the history of the village best forgotten.

Cranborne ✍

'Nowhere in Dorset is there a place so sleepy as Cranborne,' remarked author R.K. Palmer when he walked down the centre of the main street in 1950, reminiscent of Gary Cooper in 'High Noon', because this drab village has the appearance of a Western Cowboy Town. He met no guns but, in a quaint shop at the end of the street, encountered one of Dorset's lovable characters, saddler Ted Amey. Seventy-five years old Ted, silver hair combed into a neat quiff over his forehead, piercing eyes and a huge white walrus moustache which swept below his cheeks, was working in his shop amidst the strong sweet smell of leather and oils. It seems a trivial memory of a place so steeped in history, but the best memories are like that.

The magnificent Manor House, dating back to Henry VIII, has been greatly improved by the Cecils who became Lords of the Manor during the reign of James I. The first Earl of Salisbury added exquisite Jacobean porches.

Like many other Dorset towns and villages, Cranborne's great days are in the past, when it was a garrison for troops who protected the kings who hunted over the Chase, and it had a population comparable with London and Durham. Once it had a market every week and staged two fairs a year.

Cranborne tanners shod the people of Wimborne and Blandford, and weavers provided their clothes as well as sustenance from eleven breweries.

As Cranborne, a thousand years old, slumbers on in old age, let me tell of another sad Dorset love story.

The Lord of the Manor in Saxon times, one Brictric son of Algar, spurned the love of a Flemish Princess called Matilda, so she turned her attentions to a tall, corpulent, balding figure of a man called William, sixth Duke of Normandy. She married him and he became The Conqueror. When Matilda returned to Cranborne she played the woman scorned and had Brictric cast into a dungeon.

The Crichels 🌿

The remote and lovely village of More Crichel, in rich farming country, situated between the little rivers Gussage and Tarrant, became famous after the last war because Lt. Cmdr. George Marten and his wife Mrs. Mary Marten, wealthy landowners, struck a blow for English freedom in a long case to free agricultural land taken over for use as an airfield.

The name Crichel re-echoed through the corridors of Westminster and brought down a Minister of Agriculture.

More Crichel and neighbouring Long Crichel are now free of the noise of aircraft, and the runways of the Tarrant Rushton aerodrome have have been cut asunder by the plough. Crichel House, the home of the Martens, is one of the loveliest residences in the country, reflected in a 30 acre lake.

When fire demolished the original house in 1742, the then owners removed all the village except the church so that, in the rebuilding, the house would have a perfect setting, amongst green slopes and terraced gardens.

However, its beauty could not have been appreciated by Princess Charlotte, daughter of George IV. Whilst persecuting his wife,

Queen Caroline, he took the child and literally imprisoned her at More Crichel. The sad royal domestic upheaval ended unhappily – Charlotte died at the age of 21, giving birth to a dead son. Had she lived to become Queen of England, there might not have been a Victorian era.

The church of More Crichel, new in Italian style, has a brass portrait of Isabel Uvedale who gave her husband 13 children 'to his joy'. A quote that will cause much amusement today.

At Long Crichel, three miles away, a skull found in 1939 had signs of an operation carried out over 4000 years ago. The surgeon's knife had been a sharp edged flint in performing a trepanning operation to relieve pressure on the man's brain. We do not know whether it was successful.

Dewlish

The chalk hills form a valley to allow the Devil's Brook to flow past under a little arched bridge, and the mixture of dwellings on the slopes form the village of Dewlish. A pleasant place where it would appear nothing ever seems to happen, yet prehistoric elephants once roamed on these slopes. We may never have known of it had it not been for a busy little mouse and a diligent geologist who, in the 19th century, found a mousehole in the chalk face filled with sand. Excavations were made and not only was a layer of sand discovered, but the remains of long forgotten animals. The bones of elephants thought to be 17 feet tall are now in Dorchester Museum. The Romans lived at Dewlish, but those great animals roamed here long before the Ice Age.

The Norman church is approached through an avenue of yews so thick and matted at their tops, that they blot out the sun and form a dank, darkened nave reminiscent of the lonely depths of the Burmese jungle.

Durweston

Beside the River Stour, two miles north of Blandford lies Durweston. To reach it you cross the narrow stone bridge which forms a T-junction with the A.350 Shaftesbury road. The bridge was built in 1795 by the Portman family who owned Bryanston, which is downstream and their housing estate is part of the Durweston village which spreads between the high ground and the water meadows.

In Domesday it had three vineyards and the 500 year old church has a curious sculpture over the door showing one man holding a three legged horse and another man showing a horseless leg. He is thought to be St. Eloy the patron saint of blacksmiths, who in church windows is frequently depicted as a farrier because, according to legend, he once removed a horse's leg to shoe it and afterwards replaced it.

St. Eloy acquired great skill in working precious metals. He worked in Limoges and when the king required a golden throne, Eloy went to Paris to carry out the work, but the king had supplied enough raw material to make two thrones. When the king paid Eloy for his fine workmanship, Eloy produced the second throne. The king, pleased with Eloy's honesty bade him swear allegiance, but he was unwilling. The king did not force the issue saying 'I would rather have the word of Eloy, then the oath of another man'. He made the goldsmith Master of the Mint. He became Bishop of Noyon and died in 659 AD.

In spite of its position by the Stour, with Stourpaine standing on the other bank, it is not a village which impresses with its beauty or architecture. It is, however, the backway into Bryanston Park and School.

Bryanston was originally the town of Brian de Lisle, a baron in the reign of King John. After a long ownership by the Rogers family, it was purchased by Sir William Portman who took part in the suppression of Monmouth's rebellion in 1685.

The present mansion, Georgian style in red brick, is seen at its best when you approach from the Badbury Rings road, descending the Blandford Hill.

It stands on a hill in the centre of the great park and is now the Bryanston public school. A magnificent setting for learning in these peaceful woods and the boys, like those at Canford further south, have excellent rowing facilities on the Stour.

Norman Shaw designed the building for the second Viscount Portman at the turn of the century. The main entrance gateway at the Blandford bridge is an imposing 18th century structure by Wyatt.

Evershot ॐ

Leland described it as a 'right humble towne'. From a spring at St. John's Well rises the stream which eventually becomes the Dorset Frome, setting out on its 35 mile journey to Poole Harbour.

Wild boars once roamed here and the Anglo Saxon word Edfor (wild boar) and the early English holt, meaning thicket, give us its name. The spring encouraged early settlers but it did not become a parish in its own right until 1974.

Although it only has a population of about 200, it is a deceptive place, and has shops, bakery, street lighting, pavements, school, a doctor's surgery and some beautiful lasses. One such young lady with the largest and most lovely eyes I have ever seen, who was leading two ponies, kindly showed me the road to Yetminster.

Evershot is the second highest village in Dorset – about 700 feet above sea level – which has an oddly urban look as a result of 19th-century facelift producing raised pavements and bow shop-fronts built onto much older house faces of yellow and grey limestone.

During the railway boom in the 19th century, at a time when the railway authorities were actually giving stations away, Evershot was provided with a halt at Holywell, nearly two miles away.

Farnham

They ask you to drive slowly through Farnham, but I cannot imagine anyone wishing to rush through this lovely village of white cottages dominated by thatch, lest he miss but one lovely garden ablaze with the old fashioned flowers of the countryside.

It is not the typical Dorset village beauty which has made the name Farnham famous all over the world, but a museum founded by a great Victorian, Gen. Pitt-Rivers, a wealthy landowner in the district. It was he who restored King John's Hunting Lodge at Tollard Royal.

The centre piece of his vast collection, which covered man's growth from savage days to the 19th century, were items excavated from nearby Woodcutts. A perfect example of a Romano-British village, with models of the site at the time of occupation.

Amongst the objects found were flint implements of the late Stone Age, and Roman coins. There were also skeletons of men and children who had died violent deaths.

The vast general collection included regalia of savage tribes and an agricultural section followed the development of farming implements.

This important and unique museum was housed in a building originally built as a residential school for gypsy children in the 1840s by the Rev. John West, but it is now closed and the great collection sadly dispersed. However, the Woodcutts collection can be seen in Salisbury Museum.

The church hides on a hillside behind the village cottages. It is built of local green sandstone and knapped flint, with an attractive 14th century tower. Near the entrance is the ancient village well, protected by a thatched lych gate style shelter.

FARRINGDON — JOHN BAKER

Farringdon

Little is known of the village called Farringdon. It died hundreds of years ago and all that is left is a broken chancel arch in the centre of a large field, between the 18th century Came House, and Herringstone House of Tudor vintage, in the peaceful 230 acre Came Park, near Dorchester.

The Dorset poet, William Barnes, when rector of Came found inspiration beneath the shadow of this peaceful arch and wrote:

> 'I seem to see the church's wall
> And some grey tomb below a yew,
> And hear the churchyard wicket fall
> Behind the people passing through.
> I seem to hear above my head,
> The bell that in the tower was hung;
> But whither went its iron tongue
> That here bemoaned the long lost dead?'

When I visited Farringdon in the freshness of an early spring morning, two fine horses had found it first and seemed aggravated by my intrusion.

Ferndown

The Saxons called if Fiergen – the wooded hill, but whatever heathland charm Ferndown possessed has been destroyed in its transfor-
mation to a dormitory for Bournemouth. Let me quickly add, a very
high class dormitory, but described as the 'largest and fastest growing village.'

In fact with its busy and important shopping centre built around
a crossroads on the Wimborne to Ringwood road, and a major
industrial estate, it has now reached town status and has its own
council and proudly supports the office of Mayor to rule over nearly
1500 people.

Nothing seems old in this thriving young community. Schools,
church and hotels are modern, even the romantically named
Smugglers Haunt is very new, but Ferndown's name is carried by
one of the most famous golf clubs in the south.

It is strange that heathland ferns played no part in the naming of
the village. At the time when the English archers were fighting the
French at Crecy it was known as Fyrne and later in that century
became Ferne.

Fiddleford

A mile or so down river from Sturminster Newton, hiding from
the main road traffic is Fiddleford, with what must surely be the
most picturesque of all the Stour mills. In the fields around, the
young William Barnes worked. His poem *Leaves*, although written
at Mere much later was probably inspired by this portion of his
beloved Stour. Because he chose only to write of beautiful things
he ignored the seamy side of life in the vale, but a contemporary of
his, Robert Yound, tells of drunken brawls and even murder.

Fiddleford Mill it would seem was a hiding place for contraband
liquor, and from these stocks the factory workers at Sturminster
Newton crazed their brains and fought in the streets.

Fiddleford has the most spectacular medieval Manor House interior in the county, built about 1380. The two storeyed solar wing and half the hall to the east of it remain. Their open timber roofs are spectacular. In the 16th century the solar wing was extended to the north, and the hall re-modelled. One of the features of this fine building is a plaster ceiling of the typical Tudor style.

The mill house stands alone reflected in the mill pond which fills from the Stour as it cascades over a weir. It is a beautiful setting, and fishermen cast out beyond the Stour's own water plant, the yellow clote, and picnickers laze within sound of the weir.

No longer does the old mill rumble as it ground the corn, but the last miller showed me the strange inscription chisled into the wall of the building in 1566. It is an exhortation to the miller and reads:

> 'He thatt wyll have here any thynge don
> Let him com fryndly he shall be welcom
> A frynd to the owner and enemy to no man
> Pass all here frely to com when they can
> For the tale of trothe I do always professe
> Miller be true disgrace not thy vest
> I falsehod appere the fault shal be thine
> And of sharpe punishment think me not unkind
> Therefore to be true it shall the behove
> (To) please god chefly (that liveth) above.'

Fifehead Neville

The Romans lived here but a Saxon thane gives us part of the name. A hide was originally the amount of land which would support life for a free peasant family and, although its size varied, in Wessex it was 48 acres. So Fithyde was a village of 240 acres, in the time of the Domesday Book, but today it is nearer 1500 acres in size.

William de Nevill, who came over from Neuville in Normandy, gave the village the second part of the name.

Foundations of a Roman house were excavated there and tools and jewellery discovered can be seen in Dorchester Museum.

Amongst those who chose to live in this quiet village was the mother of the Rev. William Barnes.

One of the few surviving pack horse bridges in the country crosses the little river Divelish. A supreme example of medieval craft, but it is a very long time since the last laden pack horse crossed this narrow bridge.

Parts of the church have roots in the 15th century but the nave is 18th century, with a panelled pulpit also of that era. An old twisted yew tree forms an umbrella over the lych gate and in the churchyard is one of the largest table tombs I have ever seen. It is about 20 feet by 15 feet and nearly 6 feet tall.

Fleet 🦪

Fire and storm have played disastrous roles in the story of Fleet, a village beside the Fleet lagoon and in the shadow of the towering Chesil Bank. In 1824 the Bank took leave of its protective role in the great storm which destroyed Weymouth promenade, and caused the water to rise over twenty feet in the nearby village of Abbotsbury.

Buttery Street at Fleet was washed away and the whole of the church except the chancel was destroyed.

Fleet, another Dorset village where truth and fiction blend is the centre of J. Meade Falkner's, *Moonfleet* a tale of old smuggling days. The Moones or Mohuns who originally came over with the Conqueror, who also play an important role in the fictional tale, lived here, and in the vault beneath the church the contraband was stored beside the coffins. In the 1920s an underground passage was discovered, 3 feet below the ground and 5 feet high, through which it is supposed the smuggled goods were brought.

Buttery street was rebuilt and the Countess of Ilchester provided food and clothing for those who had lost all.

In 1930 the cottages were modernised but later in that decade were all destroyed by fire except one, and once again they were rebuilt.

One of the Mohum family died in a blizzard in 1757. He was frozen to death whilst returning from Weymouth.

Fleet House, now a popular Hotel, dates back to 1603 and was supposedly built by the Mohuns who must have been very productive. A plaque in the old church commemorates Robert and Margaret Mohun. She died at the age of 90 years having given birth to 17 children.

The great storm of 1824 swept a 95 ton sloop on to the Chesil Bank above the village. It was hauled down into the Fleet Water and towed to Weymouth with the loss of only two lives.

A more incredible incident took place in a storm 15 years later when a 500 ton vessel was thrown right over the highest part of the Chesil Bank, nearer Portland, and floated off unharmed into the water now known as Portland Harbour.

Fontmell Magna

The old gossip tree in the heart of Fontmell Magna, around which the villagers met for 250 years, was defeated in old age by Dutch Elm disease and the disastrous drought of 1976. Chopped down with much ceremonial, a plaque was unveiled on the site and young lime tree planted as a replacement.

There was a legend which said that anyone taking part in the old tree's destruction would have bad luck, and at least one villager gave it thought when, shortly afterwards, 70-year old Frank Hewkins, a bellringer, tugged on his rope and the wheel of the tenor bell shattered above his head.

It was only two years previously that the restored bells rang out for the first time in 20 years. In 1843, Sir Richard Glyn provided a school and the young girls had to sew shirts for their benefactor, but in 1975 the women of this sleepy, lovely village struck a blow for women's liberation by forming a women's cricket team.

On the hill above Fontmell (the steam by the bare hill) are traces of our first farmers, the strip linchets where English agriculture was born.

The elegant church is partly 15th century, proudly displaying in the graveyard a yellow stone commemorating the winning of the Victoria Cross by Lt. Philip Salkeld, who was killed whilst leading the party who blew up the Cashmere Gate, in the siege of Delhi in 1857. He was only 24.

The story is in the best traditon of those Empire buildings days. With five comrades he crept up to the gate at dawn on September 14 1875 to commit the 'act of glorious heroism', which was to cost most of them their lives but made the capture of Delhi possible. Before Philip Salkeld could apply the slow burning match to the powder bag, his arm was shattered by gunfire. A sapper named Burgess died in a second attempt and finally another sapper, of the name of South, successfully carried out the deed. He and the bugler were the only two who survived. Salkeld is remembered on a stone in the peace of Dorset, but his body was buried on the stony, sun-scorched ridge, a waterless, wearying place which the British held for over 100 days.

Forde Abbey

There are many whose great joy in rambling around villages is the visiting of old properties, and Forde Abbey is a delight to all who venture into this part of Dorset close to the Somerset border. This is no sad ruin; no broken arches silhouetted against the sky, but a place that has been lived in since the 12th century, with a magnificent house standing in a quiet valley and the river Axe gracefully gliding past the lawns.

The monastery was founded in 1148 by the Cistercian order. One of the most colourful of Forde's Abbots was Baldwin, a man of humble birth who rose to become not only Abbot of Forde but later Bishop of Worcester and succeeded Thomas a Becket as Archbishop of Canterbury. After rallying support for a crusade throughout the country in 1188 he set out with King Richard (whom he had crowned) two years later on the Third Crusade, and died when disease ravaged the crusading army in the Holy Land.

The last Abbot, Thomas Chard, who died in 1544, did much to beautify Forde and his re-constructed cloister and refectory remain as he left them.

It became a private house 400 years ago and a chain of families with illustrious names have resided there. At the Dissolution the Abbey was granted to Richard Pollard and from his family it passed to the Pouletts, Roswells, Prideauxs and then to the family of Gwyn.

During the Civil Wars it belonged to Sir Edmund Prideaux, Attorney General to the Commonwealth, and its ancient walls were spared. It was this Prideaux who employed the famous Inigo Jones to make changes and alterations to the building.

His son had the misfortune to be a friend of the Duke of Monmouth, a friendship which cost him a spell in the Tower until he had paid a ransom of £15,000 for being an accessory to Monmouth's Rebellion.

Sir Francis Gwyn inherited the estate by marriage in 1702. He was Secretary of War to Queen Anne, who for services rendered presented him with the celebrated tapestry copies of the Raphael Cartoons, the originals of which are in the Victoria and Albert Museum. They were woven at Mortlake.

Incidentally, another set of Flemish tapestries, purchased in the Prideaux era from the sale of effects of King Charles I, are placed in special settings designed by Inigo Jones.

Early in the 19th century the house was rented by Jeremy Bentham the philosopher. Today it is open to the public on a limited basis, and is worth a visit.

Frampton

Plumbers are traditionally known for forgetting their tools. No doubt the people of Frampton on April 20th., 1796 wished their plumber who was repairing the lead on the church roof had stayed away altogether because on that day he produced sparks which caused a fire in some straw and before it could be controlled 43 houses west of the church were destroyed.

Frampton reminds me of Mrs Caroline Norton, a lady well known in society circles in London in the 19th century. She was a Sheridan and frequently came to the family home at Frampton where she met William Barnes, the gentle parson whose poetry was becoming popular.

So impressed was she with William that she took him under her wing and introduced him and his work to London society.

William attended house parties at Frampton, but although his wife was never invited I am assured that there was never any cause for scandal. It was one of this famous lady's platonic friendships and if there was any loving intent it was not on the poet's side.

I make this point because after a lecture by Dr Alan Chedzoy in 1983 on the subject of Barnes and his friendships I reported that there was a hint of an affair to the annoyance of some members of the Barnes Society who were on the receiving end of the lecture.

The church is full of memorials to fighting men. An effigy of Rear Admiral Sir John Browne who helped defeat the Spanish

Armada lies on his tomb. He is wearing tilting armour and through his vizor his moustache is visible.

There is also a bust of Richard Brinsley Sheridan who was killed in action at Cape Colony in 1901. Below the bust is his sword, with South African medal attached, crossed with that of his brother William Temple Sheridan who was killed at Loos in 1915.

A plaque records that from this village of only 300 people, twenty one men made the supreme sacrifice in the 1914-18 War.

Those searching for pretty villages could tarry awhile at Frampton, a gem in the Frome valley.

It was an ancient British settlement and the Romans left fine tesselated pavements.

The present Post Office was once the Gatehouse to the Frampton Estate, and the Wessex Barn, now a guest house was formerly a coaching inn called the Red Lion. The old school has been turned into three dwellings and houses still exist which housed the men who came to build the railway in 1840.

Godmanstone ✿

Tradition has it that King Charles II stopped at a blacksmith's forge in Godmanstone and requested of the smithy a glass of porter. Quoth the blacksmith, 'I cannot oblige you Sire, as I have no licence.' Then said the King, 'From now on you have a licence to sell beer and porter.' I doubt whether the landlord will oblige with porter today, but you can still buy a glass of fine ale in the forge where horses once stood to be shod, but now there is a 20ft. x 10ft. bar invitingly comfortable and cosy. Neatly thatched with a colourful sign depicting a smithy at work, the old Smiths Arms – built of mud and flint – claimed itself to be the smallest pub in England.

In 1982 the licensee of the Nutshell at Bury St. Edmunds challenged the claim. The rival landlords decided to settle the matter with a football match which the Nutshell won, as they did the return match. For some reason there has been no further game, but the Nutshell is recorded in the Guiness Book of Records as the smallest inn. Perhaps, however, the Smiths Arms is the most beautiful, standing on the banks of the river Cerne, which gently flows past and visitors sit at picnic tables and feed the Muscovy ducks who always play there.

The village nestles under Cowdon Hill and the church has seen worshippers for 800 years.

66

The Gussages 🌿
All Saints, St. Michael and St. Andrew

A brook runs through the Gussages, All Saints, St. Michael and St. Andrew. All Saints, the largest, has a church mostly new, but three old bells hang in the 14th century tower. The village inn, which used to be called the Earl Haig, now bears the more rustic sign of The Drovers. Inside, the bar – with sagging beamed ceilings supported by wooden pillars, is warmed by a great open fireplace into which logs are fed from the chimney nook. But a surprise awaits you when you wish to spend a penny. The luxury toilets are more akin to a five star hotel.

Before St. Michael is reached, the road crosses the old Roman road, Ackling Dyke, and then runs into the village where church and chapel stand side by side on a hillside. Old bells hung in the church tower are dated 1350. Two of them, cast in the year Queen Elizabeth I died, bear inscriptions 'Feare God' on one and 'Hope well' on the other.

Gussage St. Andrew has a charming church in a field. A 12th century edifice with ancient murals is behind Chapel Farm. Although heated by electricity, the illumination is by soft candlelight.

Hammoon 🌿

A road flanked by willows and 'liable to flooding' crosses the river Stour before entering this glowing garden hamlet. The church, begun in the mid-13th century, has had its antiquity disguised by some fairly bizarre additions, like the little belfry installed in 1885 which would look more at home on a stable up nearer Wincanton, and a 15th century reredos discovered in the yard of a dealer outside London in 1946 and secured for the church by a benefactor. It is made from Ham Hill limestone and depicts the Crucifixion and three Apostles.

A few yards away stands Hammoon Manor, now become a farmhouse, a front-line contender for the title of the most pleasing house in Dorset.

It was built around 1500 with thatched roof and has Tuscan columns and mullioned Tudor windows. A Purbeck limestone porch of classical proportions was added a century later and the handsome sycamore, which stands in front of this desirable residence, adds the finishing touch – solid, dependable, embodying all that may be meant by 'roots' in the genealogical as well as arboreal sense.

The Saxons called it Hamm (home), but a Norman who followed the Conqueror to England was presented with the village which became 'the home of William of Moion'. Ironic that this Norman came from Moyon in the Contenin Peninsula to invade us, an invasion which we repayed 900 years later when our D-Day troops landed on French soil with William of Moyon's birthplace on their right flank.

Hampreston 🐦

This little hamlet, on a road which leads to the Stour, has a dour Victorian appearance analogous to a 19th century village painting, but it is old. In the Domesday Book, it was Hame (meadow) and the Preston derives from the village of the priests.

The parish accounts have amusing entries. In an effort to keep pests and vermin down, they paid 2 pence a dozen for dead sparrows, 1 shilling for a fox, 4 pence for a hedgehog and 1 penny for rats.

Once it must have been a village with little feeling for mankind. In 1716, 1 shilling and 6 pence was paid to remove a dying soldier out of the parish, and similar sums were paid for the removal of 'travelling women' who were near their time – so that they should be no burden on the community.

Many interesting burials include 'a certain soldier of Liftenant Generall Cromwell', the 'grant tyrant', who drowned in the river at Ham in 1644. In 1759 a Henry Goldney, excommunicated from the Church of Rome, was laid to rest in Hampreston.

In disastrous floods shortly after the last war, I watched stooks of corn floating in slow procession along the main street as the swollen Stour destroyed a harvest. Housing estates are closing in on Hampreston, but the village itself has so far escaped the influx of those who enjoy village life near their work in the urban areas.

Hamworthy

The villagers of Hamworthy have gone down fighting to the bitter end to save their peaceful waterside haven. Hamworthy was doomed from the day, long ago, when Poole built a bridge across the harbour and the long straggling village became a quick way to the west, meeting the main road at Upton.

It once had peaceful harbour shores on each side, because it is a peninsula within the vast Poole Harbour, separating two small bays. Lychett Bay on one side, Holes Bay with its little Pergins Island on the other. The old timers of Hamworthy accepted the tile making factory, the shipyards and the railway which ran into the docks, but were dismayed when the growing requirement for more electricity necessitated the building of a great power station near the Town Bridge and its towering chimneys cast a shadow of gloom over the village. But worse was to follow; the waste from the power station was used to fill in Turlin Moor and the old brickworks and its clay pit pond were levelled to give way to housing estates and factory areas.

Seeking to further the commercial use of the harbour, the Commissioners filled in another large area of Wareham Channel shore to build a Roll On – Roll Off Ferry Terminal to cater for the ships which conveyed the huge juggernaut lorries and their loads to and from Cherbourg, the gateway to the Continent. The villagers watched with dismay as lorries roared past their doors during the construction, carrying thousands of tons of infilling chalk, leaving the roads and houses looking as if they were cloaked in melting snow.

Today as the cross-Channel trade increases and bigger ferry ships convey more and more vehicles, the villagers stand at their gates and watch the gaily painted, but dust cloaked juggernauts from all over the Continent pass through the narrow roads.

Hamworthy has grown into a busy suburb of the rapidly expanding Poole; its little church demolished to make way for a bigger one.

The Royal Marines have set up an important base for training and have their own 'Hard' on the shore and a holiday camping site has grown into a little town, with an inn, dance hall, shops and swimming pool at Rockley.

What the Hamworthy residents have long called the 'rape' of their village is almost complete.

In dealing with the fortunes of this village, it must not be forgotten that the Romans had an important port there and built a supply road to Badbury Rings.

One section of the community is pleased with the development of Hamworthy. Because it was necessary for the Harbour Commissioners to absorb the club house and moorings of the Poole Yacht Club, (formerly the Hamworthy and Bournemouth Sailing Club) into their reclamation scheme for the harbour's port extensions, they have not only re-sited them, but for the members' personal use, built a grand new headquarters and restaurant and an enclosed miniature harbour in which to moor their yachts. Strangely enough, few of the members reside in Hamworthy. There is no justice, or as my old grandmother would say, 'It's an ill wind that blows nobody any good'.

For the historically minded, the first name on record for this part of Poole harbour is Hamme, a Saxon name. The Normans had a more colourful name, Hamme juxta la Pole (near the pool). At about the time Anne Boleyn was meeting her tragic end, the peninsula was called Hamworthy. ('Worthy' meaning enclosure or open space in a village.)

An interesting mid-17th century brick house makes a marked comparison with the modern school and library buildings surrounding it, and the mighty power station of yellow brick and towering chimney stacks, which dominates the village. The defiant brick house is the old Rectory, a building more in keeping with the Home Counties, but totally unexpected in Dorset. Facing east, the front consists of two and a half bays each side of a deeply projecting porch. There are three big Dutch gables with 'S' curved sides, two storeys of casement windows and a third in gables. For years, the Rectory was almost in a state of ruin, thick green ivy clinging and trying to protect the walls, but recently it was restored to something of its former glory.

Hazelbury Bryan

Beside the 14th century church, which dominates Hazelbury Bryan, are dwellings some 400 years old. Miss Violet Cross from the Manor House, a benefactor of the church, gave these dwellings – restored in 1939 – to provide homes for widows and daughters of the clergy.

One thing is quickly obvious, the church has been cared for by loving hands. The beautiful lych-gate, with carved crucifix, was the work of Mr R.G. Parsons of Dewlish, and it won an award from the Civic Trust in 1969. The same craftsman made the heavy panelled oaken vestment chest at the back of the church. Another fine worker in wood, Henry Spicer, who died in 1947, carved the lectern, from black oak that had originally been piles in Emperor Hadrian's Bridge at Newcastle on Tyne. Experts say this wood must have been a tree when Jesus was on earth. A kindly lady proudly conducted me into the little vestry where photographs of these men, together with clergy past and present, line the walls. The nave still has an ancient timbered roof and the bellringers platform is above the vestry. Ringers toil at the ropes in view of the congregation.

Hermitage

Many enthusiastic lovers of Dorset may show surprise if you mention Hermitage. 'Are you sure it is in Dorset?' one such traveller asked me.

Hermitage exists, but seems delighted to be a forgotten place. Treves described it as a 'Rip Van Winkle village' lying at the foot of the grassy slopes of High Stoy, a lovely hill 860 feet high, about six miles south of Sherborne.

A greater solitude cannot be imagined for the hermitage that was here, belonging to the Order of St. Augustine, yet the monks left as long ago as 1460.

A curious landslide in 1583 caused three acres of land to slip and block the highway to Cerne.

Treves with dry humour comments 'Since this date nothing in Hermitage has moved and it is a question now if even an earthquake would rouse it.'

(HARDY'S COTTAGE) BOCKHAMPTON.   JOHN BAKER

Higher Bockhampton & Stinsford

It was an American, Dr. Livingstone Lowes, who said – when unveiling a 10ft. column of Cornish granite behind the cottage where Thomas Hardy was born at Higher Bockhampton – 'It is fitting that this memorial should have its base in the soil of this heath, for Egdon Heath is in a sense the heart and centre of Hardy's world. No other English novelist or poet has been so profoundly conscious of the roots of England, deep in its immemorial, prehistoric, Roman-Saxon past. Nor has any other so imbued his landscape (road, moors and barrows) with a strange sentience, as if they had become, through centuries of human contacts, participants in that unending life.'

The roughly-hewn column, the gift of American admirers and the cottage are about all that is worth seeing in this little place, one of the five hamlets in the parish of Stinsford, yet every year thousands of Hardy pilgrims walk down the lane to visit the cottage and garden which is rapidly becoming cloaked by the caressing leaves of the giant trees of Puddletown Heath.

The bedroom in which the author was born in June 1840, takes the afternoon sun through the little upstairs window, edged with thatch, and I visualised the drama that took place 140 years before my intrusion. The doctor who was present at the birth threw the babe aside and pronounced him dead, but the nurse picking him up said 'Stop a minute, he's alive sure enough', and that simple sentance, probably uttered in the rich dialect of Dorset, saved the life of one of England's greatest authors.

I moved into the adjoining room and sat in the window where Thomas Hardy wrote *Under the Greenwood Tree* and the view can have changed little, but if you are refused such a facility by the National Trust custodian, be tolerant. The simple cob cottage with brick facing built by Hardy's grandfather, had no foundations and 10,000 visitors a year took their toll on the cottage, which has now been substantially restored.

Perhaps it is fitting that his heart should lie buried with his first wife in a grave beneath a shady tree in Stinsford church a mile away. Stinsford is the Mellstock of *Under the Greenwood Tree* and it was to this place of worship that the Hardy family came each Sunday and of which he wrote:

> 'On afternoons of drowsy calm
> We stood in the panelled pew,
> Singing one-voiced, a Tate and Brady psalm
> To the tune of Cambridge new.'

Hilton

To the vandal nothing is sacred. Telephone booth and tabernacle receive their destroying attention in the permissive eighties, but is the situation so new?

The 15th century church at Hilton in which early 16th century panel paintings can be seen, was once famous for its ancient glass, but it was destroyed in 1730 'by some idle person'.

Hilton, a hamlet where the flint church dominates the cottages gets its name from the Saxons, who it is thought called it Heltona, from the word helde meaning tansy.

The yellow tansy which grows on the slopes above the village was once used to flavour cakes long before herbs came in little packets. So a wild bloom gave its name to Hilton, 'the village under the hill of yellow flowers'.

Two miles up those slopes is the summit of Bulbarrow, beholding breathtaking views of Dorset, from the coastal Purbecks, to Mere in the north. Over 900 feet high, Bulbarrow displays the picturesque patchwork of farmland Dorset southward where storm driven seagulls swarm around the creeping ploughs, to the north the misty, romantic Stour valley, Sturminster Newton, and Blackmoor Vale.

Hinton Martel

At the time of the Conquest, it was known as Hinetone, the village of the monks. A Frenchman called Eudo Martel held it at the time of Magna Carta. His surname meant the Hammer, probably because this was his favourite weapon in battle.

In the heart of this peaceful place, they built a large circular fountain, low enough for passing sheep to drink from. It did not please the passing historian Treves, who described is as 'just such a fountain to be found in a surburban tea garden, or in front of a guady Italian villa.' In one of his passages of dry humour, he continued 'The fountain of painted metal, tawdry and flimsy, represents a boy standing in one dish while he holds another on his head. No unhappy detail is spared: the ambitious pedestal, the three impossible dolphins, the paltry squirt of water, are all here. How this cafe chantant ornament has found its way into a modest and secluded hamlet there is no evidence to show.'

I do not know what he would say if he came back to revise his *Highways and Byways of Dorset.* In the 1960s, the old watering place had so badly crumbled that a redesigned fountain, incorporating some of the old on a new plinth, was carried out by the South Dorset Technical College. Such was the brilliance of the new stone pool and the fact that its interior was painted a lovely sea blue like the clinical interior of a swimming pool, that it would make any village sheep or farmyard duck hurry away, ashamed of their own shabbiness.

To add to Treves' disgust would be the fact that the new fountain was unveiled in 1965 by Miss Ann Sidney, the curvacious young lady from Dorset who was living proof of William Barnes' famous words in his poem *In Praise of Dorset.*

74

'An we've zome women not uncomely;
Nor asheamed to show their feace.'

Ann showed not only her face but her 'not uncomely' body to be acclaimed as 'Miss World', and she has a plaque on the fountain which reads: 'Be like Miss World 1965, Ann Sidney. Throw your coins into the fountain and make a secret wish.'

It does not say for what purpose the money is used but when I last visited Hinton Martel there was only a coke tin floating on its surface.

Hinton St. Mary

The mill at Hinton St. Mary, half a mile down a lonely lane is a place of complete tranquility, and can have changed little since William Barnes, Dorset's dialect poet, came here to play in his early boyhood, from his home just across the fields.

The sleepy Stour still reflects the mill and in summer the yellow clote, the Stour's own water lily, clusters around the banks of Dorset's main river which, in its untidiness, has little dignity but great beauty.

Here is the young river, only 15 miles from its source, bubbling with joy at the mill as it did in the days of William Barnes, an area divorced from mechanical noises. Only breezes rustling the tall reeds, the constant gurgle of water over the weir and the lowing of distant cattle can be heard.

Recently, the mill was given a French background as the hiding place in the television serial, *Fair Set The Wind for France*.

The village itself, described by Treves as an uninteresting hamlet, has a fine Manor House and church, side by side. It was rebuilt by Thomas Freke, a captain of the Trained Bands (17th century Territorials) who died in 1642, but it was his eccentric son, William, who is most remembered. A tract against the Doctrine of the Trinity, written by him, was declared a libel and he was punished and the document publicly burned in the old palace yard of Westminster. He turned his thoughts to visions and wrote *Dictionary of Dreams*. In his crazy state he became convinced that he was a prophet and secretary to the Land of Hosts – so it is amusing to know that he ended his days as a Justice of the Peace for Hinton St. Mary. He died in 1744.

HOLDENHURST VILLAGE   JOHN BAKER

Holdenhurst

Holdenhurst, carefree village with its homesteads almost enclosing a charming Green, lazing on the banks of the sleepy Stour, is a strange mother for the prosperous, extrovert resort, Bournemouth, which – like many youngsters in growing up – has shown lack of consideration for a humble parent.

Not only has the town thrust its housing estates into this rural scene, but scythed a fast spur road across the village street, to the joy of the speeding motorists. This new road cut off the portion of the village where an elderly nurses home is situated, they, in turn, showed their determination (and other things) to photographers, who watched them defiantly climb a five barred steel gate to get to their church in 1969.

Amongst the lovely houses that can be admired from seats around the Green, is Magdalen Cottage, thatched and beamed and built in 1697. Hidden is a large low listed building with inglenook fireplace, which was a lepers' hospital.

Four miles from the madding crowds on Bournemouth beaches, and a long time since the lone, local constable had to pop over to keep an eye on Bournemouth, Holdenhurst fights hard to maintain dignity and seclusion. The church of St. John the Evangelist is very modern by Dorset standards. The 2nd Earl of Malmesbury opened it in 1833.

Although Holdenhurst (Hollywood to the Saxons who lived here in their wattle huts) kept peaceful during medieval wars, William the Conqueror held it in his name.

Parish accounts show that the villagers had to pay for the repair of a road at Bournemouth 200 years ago.

Holt

A thousand years ago the Saxon word for wood was holt ... so Holt, built around a large and pleasant village green, near Wimborne, has never changed its name. Nearby is God's Blessing Green, and Pig Oak, though neither place has much to show for their strange titles.

One of Holt's greatest personalities was Benjamin Bower who, in spite of weighing in at over 34 stone, was 'lively and active'.

He died in 1763 whilst drinking a gallon of cider at an inn to ward off a fit of gout. The inn, however, was not the excellent hostelry called the Old Inn, to which hordes flock from Bournemouth to partake of the excellent food served by a family in whose hands the Inn has been for many years.

In 1185 a clerk wrote down the name as Winburneholt, but he was probably trying to underline its neighbourliness with Wimborne.

The area of Holt Forest was once well known. It was laid down during the reign of Edward I as extending between Horton, Mannington, Uddens and Holt.

Holworth

On a hill behind that stretch of smuggling coast at Ringstead and Osmington Mills is the little hamlet of Holworth. It stands on the smugglers' routes inland to Owermoigne. In fact you can only approach Holworth via a cart track. It has a little wooden church dedicated to St Catherine which looks out across the waters of Weymouth Bay, to the great whale–like mass of Portland beyond.

Once the old farm was used by the Abbot of Milton Abbey as a rest home for his monks.

Dr Robert Linklater bought Holworth House in 1887 and it is said that he regularly sent prawns to the vicar of Milton Abbey as a tithe.

Until 1954 Holworth was in the ecclesiastical parish of Milton, though at the same time being in the civil parish of Owermoigne. After the death of the doctor the Oratory was closed.

The present wooden chapel was built by his widow, who died in 1942 and the Holworth Trust was set up for the upkeep of it. A medieval tile in the Sanctuary came from Milton Abbey.

There are few graves in the little cemetery and their occupants have been mostly victims of Channel shipwrecks.

Horton & Woodlands 🐿️

The final inglorious act in the story of Monmouth's flight from Sedgemoor took place in a ditch at Horton, when a searching militiaman spotted a tattered cloak and found it concealed what appeared to be a shepherd.

Monmouth might have got away with the disguise, but stupidly he had in his pocket an item that no yokel could carry – his badge of the Order of the Garter.

The starving shivering yokel was proved to be His Grace the Duke of Monmouth. Seven days later he died on Tower Hill in 1685.

You cannot but be sorry for this unfortunate, luckless man and I think of him every time I pass the 120 foot tower of Horton, which Humphrey Sturt built as a look-out to spot deer herds in 1700.

Monmouth died when he was only 36 but a much happier and more fruitful life was led by Henry Hastings of nearby Woodlands, who died naturally a few years before Monmouth, at the grand old age of 99.

Second son of the Earl of Huntingdon, he was Lord of the Manor by his marriage to Dorothy Willoughby. He not only hunted deer with great zest, but ladies as well, and kept his amorous advances going until he was in his eighties with twice daily doses of oysters.

Says Hutchins, 'he was low, very strong, and very active, of reddish flaxen hair, his clothes were always green.'

The 3rd Earl of Shaftesbury viewed this boisterous character more kindly. 'He had a good heart but violent temper and could still mount his hunting horse unaided at 80.' He lived in the style of a Saxon thane in a Great Hall strewn with marrow bones, hounds, spaniels, cats and hawks. The table was covered with arrows and hawks' hoods. In the chapel he converted the pulpit into a larder, out of reach of the animals, where there was always a great chine of beef, a venison pasty, a gammon of bacon and an apple pie.

He is buried in Horton church, a quaint Georgian building on the site of the Priory founded there in 961. It is dedicated to St. Wolfrida, who died at Horton as the Abbess of a nunnery. It is the only church in the county dedicated to this lady.

Hurn

One of my earliest assignments at Bournemouth was the photographing of the 3rd Earl of Malmesbury at Hurn Court. You can guess it was a long time ago because the school, which took over the mansion, has long since celebrated its Silver Jubilee.

I was ushered into a large room where an aging man in a green baize apron was kneeling on the floor sorting out post, rather like a giant game of Patience. We exchanged a few pleasant words and after a while I enquired how long would I have to wait to see his Lordship. The kneeling figure spun around and shouted, 'Damn it man, I am his Lordship.'

Some years later, after the opening of an extension to the Water Works, followed by an excellent lunch in which pure juice did not figure, he telephoned me. 'Ashley me boy', he said, 'Tell me, did I say anything untoward in my speech yesterday? – but it was such a good party'. I was able to put his mind at rest and told him that he had been in his usual good form.

During the last war, Hurn Court became the HQ of the Hampshire Red Cross, of which Dorothy, The Lady Malmesbury, was President. In the fine library, tressle tables jostled with antiques to form an office beneath the magnificent chandelier.

Hurn has long been known as Bournemouth Aerodrome but once it was a village store on a crossroads with a fine Manor House, all shrouded in spring by the rhododendron forest.

Ibberton 🌿

Ibberton literally clings to the early slopes of Bulbarrow, with its church, beyond delightful thatched homes, reached by a climb of 50 steps. Turn around and there is a breathtaking view of Blackmore Vale.

When Eadbeorht the Saxon and his people set up their homes on this hillside, there was – higher up the slopes – a much earlier road trodden by the early Britons and now, 800 feet above sea level, it is a six-acre picnic place. It was the first of its kind in Dorset and one of six in Britain approved by the Countryside Commission.

Ibberton is an unusual enough name but, in the Domesday Book, it was recorded as Abristentona, later as Ebrictinton and Edbrichton.

Iwerne Minster 🌿

This is a place of dignity which seems ashamed that the great house and park became a school. Even the butcher's shop has a solid oak door and a small 'inn style' board advertising the tradesman's presence. Iwerne has retained much of its ancient thatch, one such cottage forming a backcloth to the elegant war memorial.

The village pump is canopied by a wooden shelter, and those who gathered to gossip and draw water had the benefit of a notice board which carried news and events, and still does.

The church is one of the few in Dorset possessing a stone steeple, but it must have looked more imposing before restorers, at the beginning of the 19th century, reduced the spire to half its original height. The removed stones were used for the undignified business of road repairing.

Iwerne was the home of an 18th century handwriting artist. John Willis made a fortune teaching copper-plate handwriting. His pupils came from all over the world to receive his tuition in this Dorset village.

A river rises at Iwerne to give it its name, deriving from the British word Ivo (Yew). The Saxons adapted it as 'Iwern Broc', or Iwerne Brook. It is a small river and, on its journey to meet the Stour, waters two villages sheltering beneath what William Barnes described as the Eastern Hills. Hambledon stands above Iwerne Courtney, better known as Shroton, and Steepleton Iwerne is in the shadow of fortified Hod Hill.

Steepleton is a humble place, mainly an imposing house and a church. The Norman church has an arch over its altar, and the chancel was fashioned out of the base of a Norman tower. In spring the park around the lovely house is carpeted with daffodils.

Kimmeridge

Not the most attractive village on the Purbeck coast, but certainly the most interesting. A place of stone cottages with a backcloth of steep hills; unpleasant for bathing, and the black ledges thick with seaweed have been the scene of countless shipwrecks.

The Romans mined bitumenous oil shale from the geologically famous cliffs and polished it to make ornaments and jewellery. Little discs of the shale, once thought to be 'coal' money, were actually cores from the turners' lathes and are still found.

From the 16th century, luck ran out for Kimmeridge. A harbour was built to develop a trade in alum. It failed like the attempt to establish a glass works. Neither was it to be third time lucky when a French company attempted to export the shale for lamp oil. Parisians could not stand its foul smell when burning.

In 1959, Kimmeridge struck oil – the first to be commercially extracted in the country. It has hardly become a Dallas, but until recently a nodding donkey pump on the cliff edge had produced oil for 25 years.

Kimmeridge Bay is approached through a tollgate analogous to a frontier barrier, which adds to its sinister appearance ... but it is popular with skin divers and surfboard enthusiasts.

The Manor was bought by the Clavells from Sir William Uvedale in 1554, and the Folly, built in the form of a tower near the bay, although called the Clavell Tower was actually built by the Rev. John Richards as a summerhouse in the 19th century.

Incidentally Sir William Clavell was knighted by Queen Elizabeth I for his efforts in Ireland, but his nephew was disinherited because he became a highwayman.

Kingstag 🌿

There is a legend in the Blackmore Vale concerning a magnificent White Hart which Henry III spared whilst hunting. Later his bailiff in the Vale slew the animal near a little bridge at the centre of the village. So angry was the king that he had the bailiff imprisoned and fined the whole Vale. It is, however, wrong to think that this incident led to the naming of the village, as many people in the Vale believe.

Kingstag is named after the Kings Stake, a boundary stake placed in Kingstag where the parishes of Lydlinch, Pulham, and Hazelbury Bryan meet.

Both these events took place at the same time in this little place on the river Lydden, a bridge over which is the smallest in Dorset to carry the famous Transportation sign.

The village inn does not incorporate Stag or White Hart in its name, but is called the Green Man, the traditional sign for a forester.

Kingston 🌿

This hilltop Purbeck village with two churches and an inn which I find impossible to pass, has a commanding view of Corfe Castle. Few tourists know the fairy tale 18th century love story of its founder, John Scott, 1st Earl of Eldon, who became a long-serving Lord Chancellor. Oddly enough, it all started in Love Lane at Newcastle, in the year 1751, where John was born.

Although not rich, his father managed to send him to grammar school and later, as a scholarship boy, he went to Oxford. He obtained a Fellowship on condition he remained single, but fell in love with a rich banker's beautiful daughter, Bessie Surtees. Marriage was against the wishes of both parents, so John kidnapped his sweetheart, fled to Scotland, and married her. The parents relented and they returned to Newcastle for a more fitting ceremony and John resumed his law studies.

He believed till his dying day that his wife was the perfect woman. After making a fortune, he came to Encombe House at Kingston, the beautiful property in the valley called the Golden Bowl, where they lived to happy old age. When Bessie died, he became a lonely man and followed her six years later at the age of 87.

One mystery remains. Although John built a new church in Kingston, with a magnificent tower dominating the countryside (which is a landmark), their bodies lie in the tiny, older church nearby which is no longer used for services.

Kingston Lacy with Pamphill

Kingston Lacy House, situated in a large park between Wimborne and Badbury Rings has been transformed into another treasure house for the National Trust and the public are now able to share its beauty. There must be many like myself, who on an autumn morning have stood by the lodge gates at the Wimborne end of the great avenue of trees and watched the morning sun turn the foliage into shimmering leaves of gold, with the shadows of the gates tracing patterns on the thick golden carpet formed by the leaves of many years. It is my ideal autumn picture. Somewhere beyond those gates, through the specially planted specimen trees, lies the house.

The Manor of Kingston Lacy came by marriage to a son of John Lacy, Earl of Lincoln. The manor eventually came into the hands of the Bankes family, and one of them, Sir Ralph Bankes built the present mansion in 1663.

It was quite a contrast to his father's residence, Corfe Castle.

Because of excellent documentation a lot is known of the building of the mansion. Gentleman architect Sir Roger Pratt left notebooks which not only give details of the design and building, but also name the mason and the bricklayer. That the latter came from Farnham in Surrey stresses the fact that the building was built in a style alien to Dorset.

In the 1830s the house was modified for W.J. Bankes, a friend of Byron, and extensive alterations were carried out inside.

There is a grey stone church dedicated to St. Stephen, of 1907 vintage. A lovely walk from this point brings the visitor to Pamphill, a village which clings to a hillside giving extensive views of the Stour valley and nearby Wimborne.

Pamphill has an ancient chapel built on the site of a former leper hospital. This little complex today comprises of a few lovely cottages grouped around an uneven green. At the end of a tree lined drive is Pamphill Manor from the 17th century, and 1½ miles to the N.E. is High Hall, described as a miniature Kingston Lacy. It was built for the son-in-law of Sir John Bankes.

Kinson ﷼

Tales of smugglers and their law-breaking deeds abound in the old Dorset village of Kinson, but in 1931 greedy Bournemouth took it over and, to make continuance of a fast road which bypasses the town, scythed through its twisting lane to make a main thoroughfare – savaging thatched cottages, the Manor House and the old school and schoolhouse, which were right in the path of the developers.

I watched auxiliary firemen burn down one of the last of the cottages as an exercise in 1939. Today the road runs over its foundations. Amidst the garages and shopping precincts which form the modern Kinson, they built a commemorative seat on the site of the old Pound, used in days gone by for resting cattle on the journey to market at Wimborne. The rape of this village complete, it was ironical that it returned to Dorset when the new county boundaries came into force.

There had been no attempt or desire to preserve anything of the smuggling past. I watched with dismay when they pulled down Isaac Gulliver's house, custom-built for smuggling escapades, at West Howe, in the late 1930s. When the famous local smuggler moved his HQ from the White Hart in Longham to this fine lodge in 1780, with crenellations giving it the appearance of a fortress, he had one secret room which was entered from a door ten feet up the chimney. Tunnels beneath led in all directions – one is believed to have bored as far as Parkstone. In fact, the whole of Kinson, including the church and rectory, is supposed to be undermined by smugglers' tunnels.

You have to use your imagination to understand why Kinson was such an important smuggling base. Visualise Bournemouth, Branksome and Poole without any habitation. From the sandy beaches the smugglers used paths across this great expanse of heathland to bring their contraband to Kinson. All along the way, they sank wells as hiding places should they be surprised by customs men.

84

Isaac Gulliver, the gentle smuggler who never killed a man, with his gang, ran 15 luggers bringing from the Continent to Poole Bay gin, silk, lace and tea; all harmless commodities by today's smuggling standards. Gulliver's men wore a uniform – the traditional smock of the Dorset farmhand.

In one of his amusing escapades, he feigned death, lying whitefaced in an open coffin to the embarrassment of excisemen, and kept up the pretence of his death by having a funeral at Kinson with the coffin loaded with stones. This great character died in 1822 at the age of 77, and really does lie in Wimborne Minster.

Knowlton

The ruin of a 14th century church in the centre of a pagan earth circle, built in the Bronze Age, makes Knowlton – just off the Cranborne to Wimborne road – unique. Skeletons have been found which lead some archaeologists to believe that human sacrifices took place there.

KNOWLTON CHURCH.   JOHN BAKER

Jacquetta Hawkes, on visiting the ring, remarked 'There is some peculiar influence in the air of the place, an influence which ... might be called a taint'.

I once visited Knowlton before its preservation, when the church was cloaked in centuries of bramble growth making entry into the dank smelling ruin almost impossible. The sinister atmosphere scared me and even now that conservationists have cleared the growth, made neat and safe the ruin and prepared a green lawn

85

within the circle – as a picnic place – I still feel uneasy there. It is an oppressive place, haunted by terrible death.

Knowlton was once a thriving village and capital of a Saxon Hundred. Today it can scarcely be called a hamlet. Its name simply means a tun by a knoll.

Langton Matravers 🐚

Two miles inland from Swanage, the straggling village of Langton Matravers lines a road which leads to Purbeck coastal hills. It is the largest of the villages associated with quarrying. The church of St George is a stone building, like most of the residences. It is in the Early English style and the chancel arches are exceptionally rich and supported on Purbeck marble columns, with stone bases and capitals. Much of the church was rebuilt in 1876.

The village makes a good starting point for one of the loveliest walks in the Purbecks.

Leaving the village behind, a path takes you to the clifftop and a pleasant short walk to Dancing Ledge, a flat horizontal rock face formed on the cliffside where at high tide waves dance a jig on the limestone ledge and a shallow indent at its centre forms a natural bathing pool for the timid whilst the swimmers plunge into the deep blue Channel.

Along the cliff toward St Aldhelms Head is Winspit. It can also be approached by a pleasant walk from the other quarrymen's village, Worth Matravers. A valley narrows into a deep gully cut by a stream, and on each side of this chine are disused quarry workings. These are a reminder of the days when in calm weather, barges came to the cliff face and the quarried stone was lowered by derricks onto the waiting craft which then took it straight to London.

Lilliput 🐚

Lilliput naturally reminds the visitor of Gulliver and his travels, and over the years there have been the odd, old characters sitting in the bar of the Beehive Hotel, who, probably repaying a friendly

86

pint offered by a tourist, would tell how Dean Swift came to Dorset to write his famous novel *Gulliver's Travels*.

I am assured that this is not the truth, and there is no record of Dean Swift visiting these parts.

Originally, Lilliput was called The Saltings, after the trade that was carried on there, but the new name is much more likely to commemorate that legendary smuggler, Isaac Gulliver, whose name seems to pop up all over Dorset, and not only on the coast.

It might be thought that an elegant residential area would not have taken its name from an apparently disreputable character, but we do know that he owned Flag Farm in the district, and it must be taken into account that having made his fortune from smuggling, Gulliver became a respected citizen, gentleman, and banker, and is buried in Wimborne.

Anyway, Lilliput was not always the lovely residential area we now know, and the saltings were worked until 1820. Some people will tell you that the Beehive Hotel was originally a pub built to slake the thirst of the salt workers, but the hotel was not built until a later date and was more likely there for the convenience of those who worked in the brickworks and pottery nearby, on the Parkstone boundary.

If Lilliput cannot boast of a link with the little people of Swift's famous story, it did have its own woman 'Robinson Crusoe'.

This mystery lady lived in the heart of the Lilliput Woods, in a simple thatched hut. It seems that she hated people, but lived content with the affection of her little group of creatures, which ranged from rabbits and cats to a pink cockatoo.

Miss Mackenzie had a pony and bath chair style trap, and made a small living by taking old ladies for rides in it. The Scottish lady had a mysterious power over animals, but her seclusion was eventually spoiled when a London national newspaper headlined a story about her as 'Mystery Woman of Lilliput Woods', in the early 1930s.

Residential Lilliput is in the heart of Poole's great yachting community. The exclusive and expensive Poole Harbour Yacht Club Marina has been rebuilt in the premises of a former pre-war residential club which existed on the shore of the lagoon, and on its moorings in the marina harbour is a mixture of sleek racing cruisers and expensive powered express cruisers. The marina is approached via Lilliput's own exclusive little shopping centre.

Lilliput can also claim to be the home of the youngest and oldest sailing clubs in the vast harbour.

Near the Blue Lagoon, another former private club, now the base of a powerboat agency, is the Lilliput Sailing Club, only a quarter of a century old. The club tie sports a small burgee with the letter L plainly inscribed on it which causes members of older clubs in the harbour to refer to it as the Learners Club.

At the other extreme of the Lilliput shore, is the little East Dorset Saïling Club, the oldest in the harbour. The club house is on the foreshore at the bottom of that popular viewpoint, Evening Hill, and opposite what was once Flag Farm Estate.

The club celebrated its centenary in 1975 and has always remained small and exclusive. Yet in 1933, the E.D.S.C. struck an early blow for sexual equality, by electing a woman as Commodore. Mrs. E. Sherston ruled for three years, a situation unheard of in yachting circles in those days and not all that common today.

Records of the club's early days make interesting and amusing reading. At a meeting in 1898, the committee decided to employ a pierman to look after the club pier and man the club tender. They agreed to spend eleven shillings and sixpence on his jersey and one shilling and eightpence for an inscription, together with two shillings and sixpence for his cap.

High expenditure, considering they were only going to pay him fifteen shillings a week in wages.

The meeting also decided to 'make representation to the Bournemouth Steamboat Company as to the inconvenient and dangerous speed at which their paddle steamers proceed up and down the harbour'.

That complaint has been continued for nearly a century, but today the E.D.S.C. and other harbour clubs complain of damage to craft and moorings by speeding Cross Channel Ferry boats.

As I write, the sound of saws are rasping through the last of Lilliput's woodland. Every inch of this beautiful place has been sacrificed to builders, even parts of the cliff face have been built on, and who can blame anyone wishing to come here to live and enjoy the rich sunsets over Wareham Channel and the sweet cool breezes which waft in from the bay.

LITTLE BREDY   JOHN BAKER

Little Bredy

There are places in Dorset which, because of their beauty and tranquility, are a sanctuary in any season. Such a village is Little Bredy, a place as beautiful as its name would imply. A few motorists who leave the Dorchester – Bridport road still usually miss it, but down a little path to the churchyard, where the church is almost hidden under beech trees, you are serenaded by the waters of the Bride. This is the source of the little Dorset river which rises in the grounds of Bridehead, the big house of 1830 vintage, and lazily winds down the valley, slowed by weed, never – it would seem – to find the sea, because it disappears into the ground at Burton Bradstock.

I have a memory of a society wedding at Little Bredy in the early 1930s. On a warm summer's day, the bride and groom led a procession of beautifully attired bridesmaids with floppy picture hats through the church lych gate, past a thatched rectory, to the lawns of the great house. Most of the hundreds of weddings I have witnessed have drifted from memory, but I have never forgotten that day in my apprenticeship, or the sound of the river echoing through the peaceful valley.

To add to its peace, and the pleasantness of cottages hanging with white and purple aubrietia is an unusual six-sided shelter with seats. On a canopy are the words from Isaiah, 'A pavilion for a shadow in the daytime from the heat and for a refuge and cover from storm and rain'. It was a silver wedding present to the villagers from Margaret and Philip Williams in 1933.

89

Long Bredy 🌿

A mile or so beyond Little Bredy, the westbound visitor is confronted by the white west front of the great house of Kingston Russell as he enters Long Bredy. This is the medieval seat of the Duke of Bedford's ancestors.

John Russell, the first Duke, served Henry VII and Henry VIII well and died a very rich man, acquiring a great deal of land including the great Abbey of Woburn, where the great house was built to become the home of the Russells. Today Woburn is one of the country's stately homes, open to the public, and a leading tourist attraction.

It may seem like an anti-climax to tell that Sir Thomas Masterman Hardy (Nelson's Hardy) was born at Kingston Russell House in 1769. Incidentally, Kingston Russell House is not open to the public.

St Peters Church, in the Early English style serves a parish of about 2000 acres and hides amongst the trees. Amongst the rectors was the Rev. Ironside who lived to the age of 90 and died on the same day as his wife.

Lulworth 🌿

This famous beauty spot seems not only to belong to the people of the nation, but in summer has most of them trying to enjoy it at the same time. The vast car park, when filled, resembles a nest of gaily dressed ants when viewed from the hills around, while the occupants fill the beaches of the curved cove, search for fossils on the cliff-face, and scale the grassy hills for elevated views of its beauty.

The clever ones come out of season and enjoy the peace of this unique almost landlocked cove. Lulworth has never set out to attract visitors. A little shop festooned with picture postcards and selling sweets and ice creams, a hotel and toilet facilities in the car park are about all the traveller is offered, but on the outskirts the Castle Inn is a warm and cosy hostelry where, on the bar, red beef awaits the knife and a ploughman's lunch is a banquet.

Gone are the days when yellow funnelled paddle steamers drove their bows onto the beach to allow passengers to step ashore. Now fishing boats and a few yachtsmen provide the only maritime activity. The narrow entrance, a mere cut in the cliffs, deters many yachtsmen from entering the pool scooped out of the Downs, and anchoring beneath the great cliffs, high and precipitous – as well as treacherous.

I am not sure whether the ailing poet Keats actually spent his last day on English soil at Lulworth in 1820 but, on that last fated journey to Italy, the brig *Maria Crowther* was becalmed off the Cove and, with his friend Severn, he came ashore for a while. On returning to the vessel 'uplifted' - according to Severn – he rewrote his last sonnet *'Bright Star, would I were steadfast as thou art'*, on the fly leaf of a copy of Shakespeare's poems.

By strange coincidence, Rupert Brooke – who also loved Lulworth – dropped his copy of Keats into the water when boating. He leapt overboard and rescued it, probably not knowing that from this same place Keats left England forever.

Nearby, East Lulworth is now dominated by Royal Armour Corps firing ranges. This little community of thatched cottages surrounds the home of the Welds, who came in 1641 and are still here.

A Weld built the great square castle with a rounded tower at each corner and, in the Civil Wars, it was garrisoned for the King but seized by Parliamentary forces.

The castle came to a sad end in 1929 when it was swept by fire, but it is a magnificent ruin. Today, friendly Col. Sir Joseph Weld is the popular Lord Lieutenant of the county – a jovial figure who takes a very active interest in county affairs.

Lytchett Minster

The children of Lytchett Minster and surrounding villages must be the luckiest in the country. Their comprehensive school is neither a Victorian high-windowed schoolhouse, or a modern box-like building. In fact they come each day through the woods of a lovely park to the former South Lytchett Manor House, the former elegant Ham stone Georgian residence of Sir John Lees and Madeleine, The Lady Lees.

Children clatter up and down the Victorian staircase and step out on to a lawn, which has rounded balusters forming a terrace beyond which are extensive playing fields. White football and rugby posts stand out against the greenery of the park. A setting as lovely as any famous public school.

Three generations of the Lees family have been Lords of the Manor at Lytchett Minster, and lived in the big house until the death of Sir John Lees in 1955, when they bore his body across the fields on a farm truck, drawn by horses, to the little church. The ceremony was held in the lowering sunlight of an April evening, and the villagers came to pay their respects. The house and park were sold to Dorset soon after for £10,000. Madeleine, The Lady Lees, was much loved in the village and started to produce locally made religious films which became famous. At one time, she made headlines with a roadside cafe at the gates of the big house and brought out the family silver with which to serve teas.

It was a great act of forgiveness when, after the war, she returned to Italy to see the grave of her son Captain James Lees, a Special Service man, blown up at Lussino off the Dalmation coast. On the mainland she sought out the man responsible for his death and not only forgave him, but told him he could consider himself a member of her family. The Italian government were so touched by her act that they gave her a medal for 'goodness'.

The village, now bypassed, has an inn called the St. Peters Finger. At one time it was known as St. Peter ad Vincula (St. Peter in chains). Tenants and cottagers paid their dues to the Lord of the Manor at this inn on June 29, a commemoration day of St. Peter.

It is strange that the village church is dedicated to no particular saint.

Lydlinch & West Parley

This small hamlet in the Vale of Blackmore is immortalised by a legend and a poem.

Young William Barnes remembered Lydlinch bells because their sound wafted across meadows to his home in nearby Bagber.

> 'And when the bells with changing peal
> Did smite their own folks window-panes,
> Their softened sound did often steal
> With west winds through the Bagber lanes;
> Or, as the wind did shift, would go

Where woody stock do nestle low,
Or where the risen moon did light
The walls of Thornhill on the height.
Or Lydlinch Bells be good for sound
And liked by all the neighbours round'.

The five bells still hang in the tower of the 13th century church. Beneath an avenue of trees near the church porch is an old tomb, the resting place of The Lady of Lydlinch, but no one knows who she was. On the tomb we read: 'Here lie the remains of a lady who gave to the rector of this church forever one portion of tyths arising out of Dudsbury farm in West Parley and another out of Knowle Farm in Woodlands'.

To complete the story, we have to journey far down the Stour valley to West Parley on the outskirts of Bournemouth, where the nameless Lady of Lydlinch, who had endowed Parley church, wanted her heart to be buried. Six hundred years later the urn containing the heart was dug up and placed in a niche in the outer wall of the chancel of the restored church. This lady bountiful with her heart in Parley and her body in a nameless grave at Lydlinch must have dearly loved both villages.

The church at West Parley on the muddy river bank is sometimes impassable because generations of cattle have churned up the mud. It stands proudly, with a small timber belfry, in a field. The ancient walls bear stone of Norman and Saxon origin, and the door was made when the Domesday Book was new.

Nearby is Dudsbury Camp, an ancient site overlooking the Stour, from which the Ancient Britons guarded the ford across the river.

Although Dudsbury was named after a Saxon called Dude, it was first fortified by men 150 years before the birth of Christ. Today it is still a camp, but for a more friendly people. Girl Guides fill its vast sward each summer with giggling girls singing around camp fires.

Maiden Castle

Imagining the events of the past is the greatest pleasure of visiting old places which have played an important part in shaping our history and heritage; and with some background knowledge of their history the explorer of villages may sit within a castle ruin or in a long disused quarry and in his mind recreate scenes from long ago.

At Corfe one can think of Lady Bankes and her maids pouring red hot ashes onto the invading seamen from Poole as they clambered up those steep castle banks, hear their curses and screams, and the jeering and laughter of the serving girls.

At Swanage there is the intense pleasure of sitting at Peveril and remembering how the Danish fleet, fleeing from Alfred came to a grinding halt on the submerged ledge. Today a little bobbing buoy at the seaward extremity of the ledge warns sailors of the dangers.

For me this pleasure is especially true when visiting Maiden Castle, an Iron Age fortified village, and certainly one of the finest in the whole country. It was built on the site of a much earlier causewayed camp. Neolithic defences have been uncovered below the Iron Age ramparts. The castle covers 115 acres and the enclosure within the walls measures 45 acres. The Celts expanded Maiden Castle (Mai Dun) and towered the three ramparts to a height of 60 feet with steep banks.

It has been described as the perfect site for a Celtic settlement. A hill atop an open Down where sentries could watch anyone approaching for miles around, where domesticated animals could graze on open land, land which afforded no cover for predatory beasts. Nearby, at the place we now know as Dorchester the river Frome flowed by, providing water for domestic purposes and fish for food.

To scale the ramparts built by the Iron Age settlers would be very difficult for any enemies, and entering via the four gates involved the negotiation of the overlapping ramparts. However, the castle's elaborate system of defences proved inadequate against the military skill of the advancing Roman 2nd Legion under Vespasian, during the Claudian invasion in the 1st century AD.

Archaeology has provided dramatic proof of the final desperate defence by the Durotriges in the form of hastily buried skeletons excavated by the east gate, showing evidence of sword and javelin wounds.

After using the hill fort as a temporary military outpost, the main Roman site became centred at Dorchester, and Maiden Castle was abandoned to the elements. So the walls of chalk and mud built by the celtic Durotriges tribes became covered eventually in layers of earth and grass. After the Romans left Mia Dun it was never occupied again and has remained derelict for nearly 2,000 years.

Our knowledge of the violent end of the Celts at Maiden Castle is largely due to the excavations carried out between 1934 and 1937 sponsored by the Society of Antiquaries, supported by the Duchy of Cornwall who owned the site, the Dorset Natural History and Archaeological Society and the Office of Works. This powerful and important 20th century invasion was directed by none other than Dr (later Sir) Mortimer Wheeler and his wife Tessa Verney Wheeler. As a young lad I was lucky enough to watch as, with loving care they cut away the top soil of the ramparts with the skill of a surgeon neatly cutting into a patient's flesh, and they unearthed priceless finds, building up a complete history of life as lived there over 2,000 years ago. The finds included curved iron blades (probably primitive sickles), axeheads and bone combs. 100 assistants helped each year and 64,000 postcards of the excavation work were sold to the public. The whole of this four year dig cost over £5,000, most of the money coming from fund raising.

The south of England abounds with hill forts but surely this is the greatest of them all. It is ironic that in the 20th century a communications centre was built within the shadow of the castle. The massive towering pylons of the Marconi Beam Station could send messages all over the world within seconds. I contemplated this while sitting on the southern slopes and reflected that the only communication the Celts would have had of advancing Roman troops was the awesome sight of them marching across the Ridgeway.

Few seek out this place of antiquity today and you will probably share it with bleating sheep if you are prepared to scale those grassy slopes, but I love the atmosphere of this place. Silent, and sometimes when storm-clouds scud across the ramparts, very eerie, a place deserted by man and left derelict for centuries.

Maiden Newton 🐟

In spite of its old rambling streets and somnolent air, Maiden Newton has known excitement and the rare distinction of having a

95

church which bears bullet holes from two conflicts, hundreds of years apart.

The Civil War scars are bullet holes from the guns of Cromwell's men, in what is claimed to be one of the oldest doors in England. Made in 1450, it locks with a wooden bar placed in stone grooves in the wall. It hangs on the original hinges. Hundreds of years later, a bullet fired from an aircraft during the Second World War penetrated the window.

During the Civil War, King Charles I stayed at the Rectory, and Maiden Newton had another royal visitor in 1952, when Queen Elizabeth II spent the night in the royal train, parked there prior to a visit to the West Country. Although the stop was supposed to be a secret, the Parish Council obtained permission to present the Queen with an Address of Welcome.

It is a pity that the village could not have saved the famous White Hart Inn, long since demolished. Tourists flocked to this 17th century hostelry. It had two storeys with dormers in the thatched roof. The window had stone mullions and a gateway led under the house to the stable yard.

Maiden Newton is at the junction of two rivers, where the Hooke meets the Frome.

A Roman pavement, unearthed many years ago, portrayed – amongst other things – Neptune in conflict with a sea monster. A carpet factory operating in the Old Mill closed down in the 1970s, but a new industry is the manufacture of the Porcorum Sausage, a 'posh' sausage which is being sold far afield.

Mapperton 🌿

The plague wiped out most of the village of Mapperton, near Beaminster, not to be confused with a hamlet of the same name at Almer, but it still has one of the stateliest homes in the county – a showpiece retained by one family, through the female line, for many generations.

Beech trees lead to this grand house with balustraded parapet and dormer windows in the roof, built in the warm grey-yellow stone of which much is seen in west Dorset.

It was built in the reign of Henry VIII by Robert Morgan, who was in a select company of men who were allowed to wear their hats in the royal presence, 'In consideration of diverse infirmities which he hath in his head.' The frontage of this magnificent house was added in the time of James I. Facing the house is a small stone church built in 1704 which contains some interesting continental glass windows.

Marnhull

Overlooking the Blackmore Vale, Marnhull is another of those Dorset villages best known because of its Hardy fictional connections, although it was home for the British long before the birth of Christ.

It gained its name from a Saxon called Mearna, who few have heard of, but as Marlott – the home of Tess of the D'Urbervilles – it draws thousands of visitors each year. The Manor House, Tudor-style, was given to Katherine Parr, the wife of Henry VIII who survived him.

Violence amongst sporting spectators was astir long before football supporters started wrecking opposing teams grounds and cities, to say nothing of their rivals' bodies.

Bull-baiting was held at Marnhull in the 1700s and the spectators fought amongst themselves over the qualities of the animals. These fights were continued in the home villages of the competing bulls and so much damage to property was caused that bull-baiting was stopped in 1763.

I found a tomb in the handsome 14th century church amusing. An unknown knight in armour lies at rest between both of his wives. The women although of different heights are dressed in identical clothes. Some believe the knight to be Viscount Bindon who died in 1582.

Martinstown

In 1268 Henry II granted a charter to Martinstown which allowed the village to hold an annual fair within five days of St. Martins Day. The fair, which in times past was a leading horse market and amusement fair, has been revived but the old-time custom of roasting a ram was replaced with a 'badger roast', during an event in the

1960s. The 80lb badger was caught in a snare and many villagers thought they were eating goose.

After a hundred years silence, bells in the church rang out in 1947. Five new bells were hung as a village memorial to those who died in the war. An earlier peal had been sold to defray debts.

The village fights to retain its rural charm. In 1980, the villagers were 'up in arms' because the vicarage was built in brick. Despite opposition, housing estates have now been built too.

Melbury Sampford

Picturesque Melbury Sampford was the seat of one of Dorset's most famous families, the Strangways, but although they gave us the magnificent Tudor house, the village owes its name to earlier Lords of the Manor, the Sampfords.

It was in the reign of Henry VIII that the Manor of Melbury Sampford was sold to Henry Strangways for 600 marks. The Strangways came from a Lancashire family, loyal to the Crown.

In the 16th century, Sir Giles Strangways built the present house; there were later additions at the end of the 17th century.

The house is unusual in having a tower raised well above the rest of the building, a hexagon crowned with battlements and finials and at the top a room glazed on five sides with full width windows. On the sixth side a hexagonal stair turret rises higher. It is a room built for the pleasure of viewing the countryside.

The 500 year old church is in the shadow of the house and dwarfed by it, although it is not really small. Lions and wolves decorate the tower, and gargoyles, winged and horned stand out beneath them. They are supposed to guard the tombs of those buried in the church.

The usual canopied tombs, with knights in armour made of polished alabaster are present under the arches of the tower. Eqidius Strangways shares a tomb there with his wife Dorothy.

On a table tomb is a Strangways of our time. Denzil Fox-Strangways died at the turn of the century. A Skye terrier sits at his feet looking lovingly at his master. A sword hanging on a wall reminds us of General Strangways who died at the Battle of Inkerman in the Crimea.

A beautiful feature of the church is the marble reredos depicting the Last Supper.

Melcombe Bingham 🌿

In the shadow of Bulbarrow Hill lies Melcombe Bingham. Melcome in Domesday and Melcombe Horsey in 1535, when the Horsey family owned the village. Today it preserves the name of another family – the Binghams who lived for centuries in the manor house.

In old English it was meoluc-cumb, the fertile valley of milk, and the valley is noted for its milking herds.

In 1976 the village co-operated with Ansty, Hilton and Cheselbourne in several events which they hoped would get into the Guinness Book of Records. Two of these are recorded in the chapter on Ansty, but other record attempts included the building of a single stack of 33 house bricks, sixteen villagers with legs tied together running a 20 metre course in eleven seconds, and a biggest tug-of-war, with 63 competitors on each side. The rope broke under the strain during the second pull.

Melplash 🌿

Melplash is famous in the west because it holds a leading agricultural show. But visitors will soon be told of one of its colourful sons, Sir Thomas More, not – may I quickly add – the Sir Thomas More of Parliamentary fame. The Melplash Sir Thomas was Sheriff of Dorset in the time of Henry VIII.

After what we might call today a good night out, he set free all the prisoners in Dorchester Gaol. To the surprise and anguish of warders, the highwaymen, sheepstealers and pickpockets streamed out into the streets and quickly got lost in the crowds.

On sobering up, he had to beg a pardon from the King and that pardon was won for him by Lord Paulet who, with a touch of drama more akin to Victorian theatre, demanded in return one of the Sheriff's daughters, richly dowered, for one of his sons. That is how the Manor passed from the Mores into the hands of the Paulets, and over a fireplace is their motto Aimez Loyaulte, dated 1604.

The church, consecrated in 1846, is built in early Norman style, cruciform in shape with a square tower. Today a glass screen divides

99

it into two parts. The pews have been removed from the west side to form a social meeting place, and it is laid out for a badminton court. The east end is retained for regular worship. Melplash Court Gardens are sometimes open to the public. The lovely 17th century house is reached via an avenue of chestnut trees, and in the grounds are a fine barn and a circular pigeon house.

Milborne St. Andrew

Milborne St. Andrew has many facets. Once it was a leading posting place on the Dorchester to Blandford road, and today it has turned its back on the past and looks to industry to provide labour. This ancient village has over 100 men working in small industries.

The Saxons called it Mylen-Burna – the small stream, but you can no longer hear the clack, clack of the mill. The Normans built a church and the village became Mulborne St. Andrew in 1294, but no one seems to know why part of the village is called Milborne Stileham – and that name is 600 years old.

In 1967 the church bells rang out for the first time in 30 years to commemorate the ninth century of the church.

Milborne St. Andrew is the millpond St. Judes of Hardy's 'Far From The Madding Crowd'. In the graveyard a stone records the death of William Rice who died in 1826 at 78 years of age. He was the first man who ever hunted a pack of Roebuck Hounds. Mock Georgian houses on the hillside have blended well with older properties.

Milton Abbas

Milton Abbas, in a deep valley amongst the chalk hills, and the nearby Abbey, are Dorset's showpieces. The one-street village, with some 40 identical cottages built like dolls houses and evenly spaced each side of the wide road, was built 200 years ago as a model village by Squire Joseph Damer, who wanted to erect a mansion near the Abbey, at that time surrounded by an old village.

To obtain his seclusion, he built the new village of Milton Abbas just out of sight, and then destroyed all traces of the old village except one cottage. The chestnut trees, which were a feature of the new village, have now decayed but the neat lawns in front of the cottages lead past pub and church to a beautiful lake in the valley, where in summer swans and waterbirds play in the shadow of the high, well-wooded hill on the lake's distant shore. No Dorset lake is more tranquil, yet, in a certain wind, waves are whipped up which toss the swans to and fro till they scurry ashore for shelter.

MILTON ABBAS   JOHN BAKER

The Abbey and house are side by side, as they have been since 1786, in a green valley ringed by hills. A place of solitude and stillness shut off from the noisy world but, walking around the Abbey, it is well to reflect that the old village once stood on these green lawns. It was a place of many streets and taverns and a brewery of great renown, as well as having a grammar school founded in 1521 – in fact it sounds like a village after my own heart.

A thousand years ago, Athelstan, the first king of all England, founded the Abbey. It was destroyed in 1309 and rebuilt in the 14th and 15th centuries. In recent times, the mansion has served as a faith-healing centre and is now a modern public school, made famous as the setting for the television serial *To Serve Them All Our Days*.

An interesting story concerns Dorset's new resort, Bournemouth, handed to the county in the change of boundaries. The story is a modern miracle.

It appears that a very young John Tregonwell fell from the top of the Abbey church tower, but was saved from death because his petticoats billowed out and formed a parachute. The plaque commemorating this drama does not record that John Tregonwell, who founded Bournemouth, was his direct descendant. Had the first John died, the history of Bournemouth might have been very different.

Minterne Magna

One of the last corners of old England is this little village which appears subservient to the Manor House. Mellowed stone cottages with climbing roses around the doors are dotted around a twist in the road where high trees hide the Manor. Yet it is but a few steps from the little church with its front door so close to the road that one pace could put the unwary visitor under a bus.

No bungalow or new dwelling has dared intrude in this, the village of the Digbys. On a crisp sunny February morning there were giant snowdrops, profuse and Persil white around the graves in the neat churchyard. A new, small stone depicting an angel kneeling was enhanced by the sun shining on this humble grave, but, inside the church magnolia-washed walls were covered with monuments – ornate, pompous and overpowering, which needed the vast setting of a cathedral to be viewed at their best.

They are reminders of the famous families who have lived in Minterne. There are Churchills, and Napiers and Digbys. I was even walking on Churchills beneath engraved flagstones. In the gloom I read of Sir Nathaniel Napier, who built the Almshouses in Dorchester, remembered on an over-elaborate monument he designed himself. On another wall the story of Charles Churchill who, at 13 years of age, was page to Christian, King of Denmark, and at 16 a Gentleman of the Bedchamber to Prince George. After a distinguished military career, he fought alongside his brother, the Duke of Marlborough at Blenheim. He died in 1714 at the age of 56.

Commemorated in brass is Admiral Sir Henry Digby who commanded HMS *Africa* at Trafalgar and received the approbation of Nelson. He died in 1842.

Minterne, the Great Hintock of Hardy's world, is beautifully wooded and surrounded by great hills, lying in a dip between High Stoy and Dogbury Hills. The view from High Stoy is breathtaking, and on a clear day the Bristol Channel can be seen.

Outside the ornate entrance to the Manor, I remembered a character who long ago was always in trouble because he refused to touch his forelock when his Lordship passed in his carriage. He was featured in a television documentary. He must have been a strong-willed character, because I felt so humble here I would have touched my forelock to anyone who had passed.

Even the village entertainment has an old world flavour. On the church notice board it was announced that girls from a Sherborne School would be singing madrigals.

Moreton

If T.E. Lawrence, Lawrence of Arabia, who consolidated the Arab peoples during the First World War and made possible Lord Allenby's triumph in Palestine, had not chosen to retire to a cottage at Clouds Hill, in the heart of the Great Heath, Moreton, peaceful village on the banks of the Frome, would scarcely be known.

However, in 1935 his love of fast motor cycles caused his untimely death on a quiet Moreton road, and the world was soon aware of this little place. The mysterious man of many roles was buried in Moreton churchyard and on his coffin was inscribed 'To T.E.L., who should sleep amongst kings.' His grave has a simple stone carved by Eric Kennington, and a magnificent reclining figure of Lawrence in Arab costume, with his head resting on a saddle – by the same artist – has pride of place in the ancient humble church on the wall at Wareham, a church which Lawrence loved and did much to help its restoration. They say his ghost has been seen wildly riding a motorcycle through the Moreton lanes with Arab robes flying out behind him.

Moreton church is full of daylight and has fine engraved glass chancel windows by Laurence Whistler.

The Manor House is the seat of the Framptons, but it is the cottage at Clouds Hill to which tourists flock. The humble Lawrence abode, now cared for by the National Trust, is colourful in May when rhododendrons bloom around it. Simply furnished, it has a

103

couch, table and armchair and upstairs, in the music room, is a gramophone and 800 records with the accent on Beethoven, Schubert and Mozart.

Lawrence, it would seem was to have no peace even in death. In 1940 a bomb fell on Moreton and damaged the north wall of the church, demolishing part of it. It was not properly rebuilt until 1950.

Mudeford ✤

Twice in its history, Mudeford almost became a famous resort, and this proud village with a fascinating sand spit where fishermen live, was accepted with some pleasure by Dorset when, in the change in county boundaries, it was lost to Hampshire.

It might have been a leading resort popularised by King George II but, having inspected it, he moved on to Weymouth where he established sea bathing. Later Tregonwell came and paddled on the Mudeford shore, but went away and founded a resort further west called Bournemouth.

However, Mudeford – which takes its name from the tiny river Mude, the little known third river to use Christchurch harbour as its estuary – has had some fame.

Sir Walter Scott and Coleridge found inspiration at Gundimore House on its shore, and the narrow entrance to the harbour has been the scene of battles between smugglers and excisemen.

Before the last war, the Spit, which bears picturesque Dutch style cottages and an old fisherman's inn, was often cut off by the tide. Developers built a great quay wall and an enormous car park to rob Mudeford of much of its charm, and the inn, where once bearded fishermen sat on wooden benches and nicotine stained walls bore dusty nets and lobster pots, now has a cosy bar and a palatial lounge but, thankfully, has not been robbed of all its old world atmosphere.

Unlike the Mudeford in Somerset which Domesday Book described as a muddy ford, the Dorset Mudeford comes from the Saxon word Muda which describes the mouth of a river.

Mudeford folk will tell you that they have no regrets that the place never quite made fame as an international resort, but in spite of the fact that it has changed beyond all recognotion, it still remains a village by the sea.

Netherbury 🌿

A narrow lane loops off the Bridport – Beaminster road and helps to give Netherbury the peace it deserves. Where the river Brit rushes under a bridge in the valley is a breathtaking view of the church high up on the hillside, overlooking the roofs of houses dotted on slopes. I first came to Netherbury in 1936 and had not been back till recently. It has hardly changed in nearly 50 years. On my first visit I was interviewing Harry Warren, a cider maker, and tasted his championship winning Champagne Cider. Today his son is still making the delicious drink.

Another resident told me that so many properties were now owned by 'townies' that he hardly knew anyone in the village. I can think of no lovelier place to spend a quiet weekend.

In the church I was reminded of the Hood family of seafarers, including Sir Samuel Hood who was with Nelson at Santa Cruz and the Nile.

Close by is Parnham House, for 300 years the home of the Strode family. Built in the 16th century and altered in the 18th, it has had many owners since 1896.

Until recently it was owned by the National Association for Mental Health but has now become a prestigious centre of furniture making and design, well known to our own Royal Family.

Nottington 🌿

Nottington was once famous for its spa. Aristocrats flocked from Weymouth three miles away to take the waters which, it is said, cured 'eruptive complaints, scrofula and loss of appetite.'

Remedial qualities in the water were discovered by accident. A shepherd who drove his flock along the Nottington Lane found that sheep which drank from the spring and splashed into the little lake, quickly recovered from a disease called scab. The water was analysed in 1816 by Dr. J.A. Pickford and in 1830 Thomas Shore built the unusual octagonal Round House to provide accommodation for those taking the spa water. It is said that he had eight sons and an octagonal dining table. The sulphurous spring water was found excellent for the skin and muscular ailments, and George III was a regular visitor.

Today no one comes to Nottington to take the spa waters, but the queer three-storey building, designed by the architect who was responsible for many of Weymouth's Georgian facades, still stands and I believe the pumps are still installed.

Nottington is in the Hundred of Culvardestre, which has become known as Cullivers Tree, but to generations of schoolboys it is Gullivers Tree.

Oborne

There can be something rather sinister about chancels which defiantly remain standing long after the church has disappeared. For example at Fleet, the chancel which defied a Channel storm lives on in the novel *Moonfleet*, but the history of the missing church at Oborne seems to be more obscure. Away from the main road at Sherborne, it is literally a village amongst the meadows with the little trickling river Yeo running through it.

The chancel of the old church stands with its graves dotted around it. Built in 1533, the building had typical Tudor style windows, and it is possible that the two earlier perpendicular window-heads in the west front came from the lost nave. The pulpit is dated 1639 and it has heavy altar rails and altar table also over 300 years old.

A new church stands on land given by Caius College, Cambridge and is dedicated to St. Cuthbert. It is all very Victorian with font and pulpit in stone.

This little place, where the river waters a profusion of forget-me-nots is a peaceful oasis, and one man who must have enjoyed its seclusion was John Shuttleworth, the rector for 57 years. He started his ministry in 1693.

Okeford Fitzpaine

One of Dorset's most attractive villages with timber-framed cottages, formed with locally made bricks, has fought to retain its rural charm and solitude. Not only have the villagers tried to stop traffic rushing past ancient dwellings, but have successfully fought to have ugly overhead electric cables removed. Twenty-five of the 18th century buildings are listed.

In 1966 much of the village went under the hammer and was sold up for £166,000 but at the wish of the late Captain George Pitt-Rivers, who owned it, the properties were sold in lots to enable residents to purchase their own houses. One old man got his three-bedroomed thatched cottage for £1500.

Close by is a picnic site, high up on the famous Ridgeway – one of the country's ancient walks, which stretches from East Anglia to Devon.

Villagers still chuckle when they retell the story of Robertson of Payn, one of the early Fitzpaines and a former landowner. He fought at the Battle of Lewes against King Henry III and was one of his captors. Analogous to a modern soldier 'borrowing' the sleeping out pass stamp in the Guard Room behind the military policeman's back, Robert of Payn and a man called Govis 'borrowed' the King's seal and set it on a document excusing them from paying dues on their estates.

The sting in the tail of their amusing ruse was the rider stating that the grounds for the special indulgence were 'their good services to the King at Lewes.'

Osmington & Osmington Mills

How one bides one's time on honeymoon is a source of fun for music hall comedians. John Constable the famous English painter whilst spending his honeymoon at Osmington, completed the painting of Weymouth Bay which now hangs in the National Gallery, and made sketches in Preston church.

Osmington itself is a picturesque village off the main road, yet authorities have chosen to paint so many traffic directing yellow lines and dots on the narrow street, that the beauty has been scarred.

Osmington was the home of the Warham family, one of whom, William, was made Archbishop of Canterbury in the reign of Henry VII and is believed to have crowned Henry VIII.

More popular is Osmington Mills on the other side of the main road, and at the end of a lane which brings the visitor to the sea is the Smugglers Inn where lobster has been served for generations. The inn was formerly known as the Crown and later the Picnic but Smugglers is a more apt name because Osmington Mills was a leading landing place for the gentleman of the night in the 18th century. The Inn began its long life in the 13th century and for many years had a brewery at the back. It was the headquarters of the famous French smuggler Pierre Latour, better known locally as French Peter.

Owermoigne

The village of Owermoigne, three miles from Ringstead Bay, has never had a pub, but such was the high incidence of smuggling activities long ago, that it probably never needed one. Kegs of contraband spirit were hidden in the church, and the rectory has a blocked up window where once the rector's barrel was smuggled in.

An odd array of bungalows and houses are left behind as old Owermoigne comes into view, with a village centre typically Dorset, but with an unhappy and violent history. Owermoigne's disgrace occurred in the 16th century. The Moygnes lived there from Norman times for 300 years. The last heiress married a Stourton and a few generations later the act which brought shame to a family and a village took place.

Charles, Lord Stourton, was in dispute with a father and son called Hartgill. He invited them to his home pretending that he had forgiven them and clubbed them to death, burying them 15 feet beneath his cellar, and covered the spot with barrels of brandy. The deed however, was discovered. Sentenced to be hanged, he pleaded for some indulgence from Queen Mary. After all he was a Catholic and a nobleman. With a wry sense of humour, the Queen ordered that he should be hanged with a 'halter of silk in respect of his quality' and they buried that fiendish murderer in Salisbury Cathedral.

In 1588 a ship of the Spanish Armada came ashore at Ringstead Bay, was plundered and the crew murdered. Timber from the ship became beams in the rectory dining room at Owermoigne.

108

French born, Theodore Janssen, once lived at Owermoigne, a man of vast fortunes hated by the villagers earning 7 or 8 shillings a week. He was an astute businessman and King William knighted him and later he was created a baronet by Queen Anne. He was a director of the South Sea Company and when the 'Bubble' burst, Walpole blamed the company and scapegoat Janssen was forced to return £250,000. He died in 1748.

Very recently, Owermoigne has become the site of a large and colourful garden centre and if you want to buy a drink, the village shop was granted an off licence in 1964.

Pentridge

From the name, it would appear that wild boar roamed this very ancient place on Cranborne Chase – in fact, it is one of the few places in Wessex to preserve its ancient place name. It comes from the Welsh: pen – hill, twrch – boar.

The village is often mistakenly said to be the birthplace of the Dorset poet, William Barnes, but his Pentridge, a small farm near Sturminster Newton, has long been obliterated from the map.

Pentridge on Cranborne Chase, like so many places on this hunting ground of old, is a little hamlet, hiding at the end of a lane off the Salisbury-Blandford road, always in the shadow of Pentridge Hill. With the heights of Cranborne Chase on the other side of the road, Pentridge could almost be said to be at the gateway into Dorset.

The first recorded name of the hamlet, Pentric, appeared 80 years before the birth of Alfred.

Piddletrenthide & Piddlehinton

The man who presented the Dorset dialect to the world, Ralph Wightman, farmer, author and broadcaster, lived and died at Piddletrenthide. In the days when the wireless was our primary source of communication, his country commentaries, delivered in dialect, were heard internationally. In 1945 I landed by aircraft on a sandy beach in the Sunderbans at the mouth of the Ganges in India, a shore reminiscent of Studland Bay, but one of the loneliest outposts in the world. The RAF had a communications centre there.

Walking up the beach, I heard Ralph's dulcet tones re-echoing through the dunes. It was an eerie experience.

The river Piddle slowly wends its way through a fertile valley of some of Dorset's richest farmland. Such was Victorian respectability that some villages along its course have chosen to change Piddle to Puddle, but not so Piddletrenthide and Piddlehinton.

Historian Aurthur Mee would not hear of the word and changed all the Piddles to Puddle, including the river's name, in his book on Dorset.

In the *Evening Echo* Bournemouth publications, *What's In A Name,* author R.K. Palmer says the Victorians could have saved themselves a lot of trouble because the word Piddle is not rude and does not mean a trickle, but comes from the Saxon word Pidelen, or pedel which meant low land on water, fen or marsh.

The Piddle Valley cooks had no inhibitions and cashed in on their strange name by producing a *Piddle Valley Cook Book* in 1977 as a means of raising funds to restore the church. The ladies of the valley and some of the landlords of the well-loved inns, produced a book of such unusual Dorset recipes that a leading London publisher, Barrie & Jenkins, discovered it, and reproduced it internationally.

In its pages you discover Una's Mother's Flaky Pastry, Rumble Thumps, Great Grandfather's Xmas Cake, Piddle Potage and Mother-in-Law's Mincement.

Piddletrenthide has one of the finest village churches in Dorset with a splendid 15th century tower and gruesome gargoyles under its battlements. The south doorway is Norman, so are the piers of the chancel arch. The colouring of the church exterior is one of its charms. The grey, yellow and browns in the walls contrast with the distant green of the downs.

An interesting story is attributed to one John Bridges, a famous silversmith who lived here in the 19th century. An iron grille which James I set above the tomb of his mother, Mary Queen of Scots, in Westminster Abbey in 1613 was thrown on a rubbish heap in 1811 when James Wyatt, who took a delight in destroying restorations of Gothic churches, had it removed. Fifteen years later, John Bridges bought it for £110 and installed it as his home in Piddletrenthide, where it remained until the late 1920s.

Piddletrenthide is a very long village and divided into three tithings. The church and manor house is the upper tithing, another group of cottages form the middle, and the third, White Lackington. Further south is Piddlehinton on a picturesque crossroads, where

110

stands an ancient hollowed oak overlooked by a church dedicated in the 13th century, but whose building is mainly 15th and 19th century.

During the 19th century it was the custom to distribute bread, mincepie and a pint of ale on Old Christmas Day, (Jan 6th). In 1838 a disapproving parson put a stop to it and the angry villagers smashed the church windows.

The floor and walls of the church chancel are out of true, a 'weeping chancel' leaning to the right. The same way that the head of Jesus rested when he was on the Cross.

Pilsdon ৯৫৯

The west side of Dorset, as it prepares to meet Devon, has never been as popular as the better known east, so it is unspoiled walkers' country and, from its heights, miles of rich dairyland can be viewed. Pilsdon Pen, 909 feet above the sea, has landscape of sheer beauty at its feet. Tall Pilsdon is a foretaste of the Tors of Devon, treeless and formed on decaying granite, but neighbouring Lewesdon Hill, 15 feet shorter, has all the character of a Dorset height, curvaceous and green. Both look south with Channel views. Pilsdon, crowned with an Iron Age fortification, is the highest peak of Dorset and both hills stand guard on the north slopes of the lush Marshwood Vale.

The village of Pilsdon is still basking in the ancient glory in that it has a house where a Royalist judge, Sir Hugh Wyndham, lived. At the battle of Worcester, the future King Charles II fled from the field and his pursuers came to this house thinking he was hiding there. They ransacked it as Sir Hugh fumed and raged in the Hall. Intelligence was at fault, the prince being at Sir Hugh's nephew's house at Trent.

Nearby is Racedown Farm where Wordsworth first started to write seriously, and the Pildson Pen consoled his sister Dorothy, who pined for her Lakeland Hills.

Pimperne ৯৫৯

The fighting Celts gave us the strange name Pimperne, the river of tree (Pimp Pren).

111

Long after the Celts had been forgotten, Henry VIII granted the Manor of Pimperne to Catherine Howard and later to Katherine Parr. Ironically, the grant in each case was for life. There was once a Queen's Walk around the village, but all traces have disappeared.

Hutchins, most famous of all Dorset historians, wrote of a maze at Pimperne which was ploughed into the ground in 1730. A fact we may never have known if he had not married a Pimperne rector's daughter, because it was she who, at risk to her own life, saved John Hutchins' papers in a fire at Wareham. Had she not done so, Hutchins' great history of Dorset might never have been published.

The gentle stream, which flows through this untidy village, is a subject of concern today. So much water is being extracted from it by the Water Authorities, that it is feared it may dry up.

In the 1970s lunches were served at the Rectory for 75p to raise funds towards clergy stipends. It is not recorded whether customers were told that the Rectory was haunted. Incidentally, Charles Kingsley was a curate at Pimperne for a short time in 1844. In a village which was the home of Henry's wives, it is amusing to note that a plaque was placed in the church by a parish clerk, who had more patience with his wife than Henry. It reads: 'To the memory of the best of wives.'

Portisham

National newspapers have not always relied on the charms of bare-bosomed young ladies to decorate their pages and entice new readers. Long before Page 3 became the aperitif to stimulate businessmen before they turned to the stocks and shares and more serious stories of the day, the newspapers of the 1930s indulged in 'silly seasons' when there was a lack of news.

Some readers will remember the famous contrived photograph of a policeman chasing naked boy-bathers in Hyde Park during a heat wave, or the antics of the public when a large turtle was set down in Trafalgar Square. The series of pictures ended with a gentleman with an eye to business trying to sell it to Macfisheries.

In such a newsless week in 1936 my colleagues filed a story saying that cat racing was taking place, with an electric mouse in the village of Portisham. The friendly landlord of the 'local' agreed to admitting that it had happened, should he be challenged.

Unfortunately the *Daily Express* thought it a good enough yarn to warrant sending a photographer, so we quickly organised several stray cats and lined them up at the inn, with kitchen scale, as if they were being weighed in.

When published, the picture caused uproar in the village.

I mention this because Portisham is a quiet, dour village and did not deserve such treatment. Set in a valley, motorists pause to look at the pretty village green and pass on to Abbotsbury. They often miss the home of Thomas Masterman Hardy who lived at Portisham from the age of nine.

The captain, in whose arms Nelson was to die, was a true Dorset man believing that the county's beer, mutton and cheese was the best in the land, and claimed that the 'beer was the best ever drank' if it came from 'Possum', his name for Portisham.

On the heights of Black Down, above the village, his memorial column stands 770 feet above sea level, plainly seen from Weymouth, where many people still believe the column commemorates the author, Thomas Hardy.

There are other monuments on the heights around the village, much older than Trafalgar days. Five huge stones stand here called the Grey Mare and Her Colts, plus the Fallen Circle at Tenant Hill and a cromlech called the Hellstone, the Stone of the Dead. Nine upright stones supporting a capstone 10 feet long was possibly the burial place of a chieftain in the late Stone Age.

Portland – Fortuneswell, Chiswell, Grove, Wakeham

Portland, a precipitous island prominence protruding into the English Channel, like a giant flint arrowhead, has been described as 'one of the ugliest sights in the world', yet from the bowels of this island of villages, linked to Dorset's mainland by the unique Chesil Beach, comes the stone which has beautified famous buildings all over the world.

Resembling a Mediterranean island, its spirit and people are alien and remote from mainland Dorset. The tiny stone cottages stepped up the slopes now mingle with homes of another age and look grey and grim in winter, but seem to smile in summer sunshine.

The islanders are a close community who marry amongst their own folk. In the quarries son follows father into the trade and few

PORTLAND. JOHN BAKER

outsiders infiltate. Pierce, White, Elliot and Comben are popular family names. Once the islanders lived by fishing and rearing black-faced sheep. Portland mutton was a delicacy, but like real Blue Vinny cheese is now a legendary dish.

Three and a half centuries ago Inigo Jones discovered the stone and used it to build the banquet hall of Whitehall Palace. From then on the men of Portland dug into the limestone with chisels and bare hands, cut out the chunks of stone which decorate such famous edifices as St Paul's Cathedral, Buckingham Palace and more recently the United Nations Building in New York. Portland, $4\frac{1}{2}$ miles long by almost 2 miles wide, is 496 feet at its highest point in the north where a former underground fort now serves as a prison, and slopes down to 20ft above sea level where its Bill meets the force of Channel storms. Several villages house just under 15,000 inhabitants, and some betray Saxon origins.

Fortuneswell, the largest, stands on the slopes facing the mainland, its gaunt church looking out over West Bay.

114

PORTLAND   JOHN BAKER

Chiswell is the old fishing centre where the men in their heavy boats still net the famous Weymouth mackerel.

At sea level Chiswell has the Chesil Bank for protection, but over the years many storms have swept over the beach swamping the houses and flooding the Square.

During such a storm I waded into Portland through 2 feet of water in the 1930s. In the darkness the sound of the waves pounding the beach and the rasp of slithering pebbles as the sea receded was terrifying. In cottages I helped carry children and old folks to upstairs rooms, and in the very centre of the Square I recall three inebriated sailors playing ring-a ring a-roses around a signpost and all falling down in the chill water.

Along Chiswell's main street one of Dorset's leading fairs takes place in November, but a worse than usual storm in the 1970s drove many inhabitants away. They may return now that expensive defence work has been completed in the Cove and the damaged houses rebuilt.

The Cove is the scene of countless shipwrecks, the last being the *Madeleine Tristran* in 1930, a large French schooner. After several years the villagers were allowed to break her up for firewood. Just around the corner from the Cove I witnessed in 1936 the incredible sight of the giant 20,000 ton liner *Winchester Castle* which had glided ashore on a calm sea. As I looked down from the clifftop at Blacknor Fort she resembled a hotel ablaze with lights as the thinning fog drifted away.

115

The gaunt Borstal Institution which was formerly a convict prison is in the Grove. When it was a prison, nearby householders let their attics so that visitors could look over the walls and watch the convicts at work. The church of St Peter was built by them and its Sanctuary is paved by Constance Kent, who murdered her young brother.

The castle of Henry VIII at Castledown is now part of the naval dockyard, but where once the great Home Fleet of old anchored in the harbour formed by a long breakwaters, now sleek racing yachts come each year to attempt speed records.

Wakeham, the locals will tell you, is the oldest of the island villages and where the road bends on its way to the Bill, right opposite the entrance to Church Ope Cove and Rufus Castle is a plot of land overgrown with brambles, but from a quarry here, now filled in, came the most famous piece of Portland Stone, the Cenotaph, known to millions as the greatest memorial to the War dead.

Avices Cottage, now a museum is just across the road. This was the cottage which features in Thomas Hardy's *The Well-Beloved*, and it was Hardy who called this strange island, 'The Gibraltar of Wessex'.

Powerstock

A village scattered over hills and dales of delightful West Dorset, with its roots embedded before history was recorded. The church is perched high on a hill with a green mound – all that remains of Athelstan's Castle, once guarding the valley. The top of the hill is the ancient hill fort of Eggardon, 820 feet above the sea. The fortification is 30 feet high and the church, Norman, built of local stone. The Manor farmhouse, built in 1700 with later additions, has been restored.

The door inside the south entrance of the church has a beautiful 15th century carving, probably taken from a monastery at the time of the Dissolution of the Monasteries. The carving shows a king holding a book and staff and a crowned female giving bread to children. They are thought to be Good King Wenceslas and St.Elizabeth of Hungary.

116

Poxwell 🌿

The 17th century Manor House at Poxwell, with stone mullioned windows, chambered porch and a unique little porter's lodge over the garden gateway, has outlived the more modern church which dominated it for many years. This place of worship with round tower and spire, unusual in this county, was demolished in the 1970s.

Built by the Hennings, the Manor House is situated in a small copse with a green hill as a backcloth. The cottages which line the main Weymouth road have been restored, and the peaceful village gives no indication of the evil events of the high Down just beyond the village, where fanatical Druids long ago made human sacrifices around a stone circle. A miniature Stonehenge with a diameter of only 14 feet.

There is an ornamental well in the village, but name derivation experts are divided as to whether Poxwell is Puck's Well, or named after a tribesman called Poca, who lived on the hill. Well coming from the old English 'swelle' – hill.

Poyntington 🌿

At Seven Wells Down, the river Yeo rises and here is Poyntington, in the far north of the county, out beyond Sherborne.

Its Tudor House was the home of the fighting Malets. Sir Thomas, born 1582, was Judge defender of the cause of Charles I, while 19-year old Baldwin Malet was killed in a skirmish near the village fighting for his king. William Malet was ordered by the Conqueror to see that Harold had a funeral fit for a king and, more recently, a descendant, Sir Edward Malet, was deputy Commandant of the Royal Armour Corps at Bovington.

The home of Poyntington's other family, the Cheneys, is now a farmhouse, but mention of it gives me an excuse to record the name of the infamous Judge Jeffreys. This hated man held one of his courts here in the house during the Assizes following Monmouth's Rebellion.

Preston ✍

It was a thrilling adventure when, as a cub scout I came to camp in the valley of the Jordan, but the little stream which enters the sea at Preston, near Weymouth would hardly be deep enough to carry out a full scale baptism. Preston's main claim to religious fame in fact that John Wesley's grandfather, old John Wesley, lived there and died in 1678.

The Romans landed at nearby Bowleaze Cove and the foundations of a Roman temple have been found. There has been a new occupation in modern times. The meadows which slope down to Redcliffe Point at Preston are covered with row upon row of caravans, necessary I suppose being so near a popular seaside resort. They do not enhance the view of Weymouth Bay as seen from the hilltop, the first sight of the blue waters of Weymouth Bay, known as the Naples of England, with Portland beyond.

The church, Gothic styled is mainly 15th century and has a quaint inscription engraved on one of the peal of 17th century bells.

'See in what a state the rich they live,
Nothing unto the poor they give.'

It was here that Constable painted his famous canvas of Weymouth Bay.

Puddletown ✍

Whenever I am asked to describe a typical Dorset community, I think of Cranborne and Puddletown, because both these large villages seem unimpressed by change and modern standards.

Puddletown was once proud to be a Piddle village but, in recent years, has changed to Puddle – not that it sounds any more dignified, but I remember the words of a resident who, when I was still a very young newspaperman, told me: 'Tis like this youngun. We do be a crossroads and the townies in Dorchester – when giving directions – didn't like having to say, turn left at Piddletown.' Under any name, it is a remaining example of Dorset over 300 years ago.

It once had the status of a town and was the 'Weatherbury' of Hardy's Wessex novels. Thatch and later style roofs form irregular patterns on the skyline. The church, more than any other in the county, has been left unchanged over the centuries except for lighting.

'Nowhere in the county will you come into closer communion with the homely spirit of Dorset past,' said Treves of the church, and today you can sit in a pew and take your mind back 300 years to visualise the farm-men in smocks sitting on the benches with their wives in homespun. The tumbler shaped Norman font to which they brought their young for christening, is still in use. Above, the gallery built in 1635 from which the choir led the singing and the porch are unchanged since the days when the ladies curtsied and the men touched their forelocks as the squire and his lady arrived to take their place in the manorial pew.

For a long time, Puddletown was dominated by the Martin family who had two manorial houses close by – at Athelhampton and Waterston. Their graves fill the south chapel.

An inn in the village is called the Blue Vinny but that hostelry will not have seen such Dorset cheese for nearly 50 years. The recipe seems to be lost, but it is claimed that it will soon be on the market again. In any case, I can assure you that you have to acquire a taste for it.

In May and June the rhododendrons of Puddletown Forest are a pleasure to behold.

Radipole 🐦

Weymouth harbour, beyond the Westham bridge, is known as Radipole Lake. A peaceful bird sanctuary and home of swans till a scheme to provide work after the First World War sent a road straight through it to the village of Radipole, at the lake's northern end.

Once a pleasant little village, known in early days to the Romans who brought small ships from the sea to a landing near where the present church is sited. This church, with a quaint Italian style bell steeple of three cusped arches, was once the mother church of Melcombe Regis, and must be the oldest building in Weymouth, some of it dating back to 1250.

119

Radipole, a port long before Weymouth, for centuries tried to hide behind the reeds and rushes of the lake. As a child, I found a visit to this little place quite an adventure, but its fight against progress was hopeless. A great pincer movement of housing estates moved in on two sides and, what was a beautiful village, is now the suburb of an important town.

Amongst the sons of Radipole were Verney Lovatt Cameron who, in 1870, volunteered to find Livingstone – Stanley beat him to it; and Henry Downton, who wrote the hymn *Lord her watch thy Church is keeping.*

Rampisham ✍

Come upon this village from the direction of the Maiden Newton – Crewkerne road (a lonely highway bleak when the fog comes down but blue with air and larksong when the sun shines) and you will be surprised by its lushness.

Set in a narrow chalk valley where beeches hide a large and somewhat straggling village, a thatched post office nestles next to the shallow ford and a public house called the Tiger's Head overlooks the point where four roads not so much run together as fall in a heap. The church of St. Michael and All Saints stands on a wooded knoll above the village with many gargoyles alarming enough to put any brewer's dragon to flight.

In the churchyard is a cross dated 1516 and a base better read when wet. Then the eye may pick out the stoning of Stephen, the martyrdoms of Thomas a Becket, St. Edmund and St. Peter, a pillar with a cock perched on top, fools, monks and two men in armour. Altogether, a village with a wicked sense of humour, but humour nevertheless.

Ringstead ✍

Where green fields reach down to the beach itself, beneath the towering cliff of White Nose, lies Ringstead in its own little bay and – being rather inaccessible – is protected from holiday hordes. Ancient cottages backed by a few modern bungalows are all that has developed here, yet it is mentioned in the Domesday Book.

East Ringstead was destroyed by pirates and its church has long vanished. Today the lobster fishermen go about their business watched by artists who gather to commit the 500 feet high White Nose to canvas. This Dorset clifftop inspired the Powys brothers in their writing.

The great Nose reaches out into the bay like a giant sheepdog lying with its head on its paws, friendly, protective and reassuring. The bay was not always so peaceful. The smugglers in the late 18th century used a thatched cottage on the shore as their headquarters for organised smuggling.

Just above the bay is a prominence known as Burning Cliff to the residents of Weymouth. Actually the burning was gorse set on fire by the shore party to warn approaching smugglers out at sea to hold off, as the Kings men were watching.

It is half way up the slopes of White Nose, a climb much more arduous than it appears from the beach. The Burning Cliffs, more recently revived at Kimmeridge, are caused by the shale-burning underground. The highly bituminous rock fires and bursts through the cliffs.

Ryme Intrinsica

No place in all England has a sweeter name – in fact it sounds as if it should be the home of the Poet Laureate, but it is not the most beautiful village in Dorset.

The one interesting fact is that the church, which dates back to the 13th century, is dedicated to St. Hypolite and there are only two such churches in all England.

As a little gem of useless information, Hypolite was born in 170 AD. I can tell you that he was the gaoler in charge of St. Lawrence, and the example set by this man during his imprisonment so impressed Hypolite, that he became converted to the Christian faith. Hypolite was anti-Papal and died in the year 236 AD.

There is an alms dish in the church which was lost in 1873 and found its way back to Dorset from Bideford in Devon in 1938.

St. Aldhelm's Head 🌿

As a child I believed that St. Aldhelm's Head, standing on the horizon at the eastern end of Weymouth Bay, was the edge of the world and if ships went beyond they toppled over. Many years later I recalled those thoughts as I climbed down the face of this bleak forbidding headland to photograph a sand dredger trapped on the rocks below, and recovering my breath discovered I had brought no film.

St. Aldhelm's is 350 feet high above the restless Channel and faces the chill south westerly winds. With its quaint tiny Norman chapel on the cliff edge, it has witnessed generations of seafaring history. The chapel, square without tower or chancel has weathered 800 years of Channel storms, and with only one small window looks more like a gun emplacement than a holy building.

The chapel stood there when a nearby cresset burned to warn lumbering galleass and swift caravel as they journeyed up-Channel. It was there when Drake and Nelson sailed by, and on the 6th June 1944, the coastguard in his lonely hut watched the great invasion fleet creep out from Portland and Weymouth in the eerie first light of day, to invade French soil. Today sleek powerboats pass, racing down to the Shambles Buoy. Bouncing on the waves of the turbulent restless race just offshore they disturb the white-winged cruising yachts proceeding to Weymouth in more leisurely style.

St. Aldhelm's Head, named after the first Bishop of Sherborne, is often wrongly called St. Alban's because generations of illiterate seamen found it easier to say and one of the countless shipwrecks on the cruel rocks at its base inspired Charles Dickens to write *The Long Journey*. It concerned the wrecking of the 758 ton *Halsewell*, an East Indiaman in 1786 with the loss of about 170 lives. Seventy four survivors were literally dragged up the cliff face by ropes and many of the dead are buried on the clifftop and some in Worth churchyard.

Salwayash 🌿

A few houses along the Bridport to Broadwindsor road with a tiny church and an inn called The Anchor seldom catch the eye of those who write about Dorset. Yet any village which has the magnificence of those great Dorset heights Pilsdon Pen (909 feet) and Lewesdon (a few feet shorter) as a backcloth must be worthy of mention.

The church on a rise is dedicated to the Holy Trinity, and prior to its building in 1887, the old church was across the road, and is now used as a school. This new diminutive building has a nave only 52 feet long and 25 feet wide. Yet the nave roof is 40 feet high and spanned by five pairs of principals and boarded with Spanish chestnut.

The beautiful coloured effect of the walls is produced by using white Poole, red Fareham, and black Broadmayne bricks.

Wood features in the church with seats of pitchpine, and chancel stalls and pulpit of oak. Two ladies, Mrs. Gundry and Mrs. Gildea carved the central panel of the pulpit. Wood for the altar screen came from Parnham Park and is cedar and deal.

To complete this building, which owes its style so much to local timber and mineral, is a Portland stone font; Ham stone features on the exterior.

Sandbanks

An expanse of sand dunes, once a shanty town at the entrance to Poole Harbour, became a millionaires' playground. Today Sandbanks is one of the most salubrious holiday colonies in the country.

Many of the shanties and old converted railway carriages, some without drainage and water, were residences and summer homes for people who had set them up soon after the turn of the century, and the last of these eyesores disappeared in the 1960s.

Today a house at Sandbanks can cost over £100,000 and every square inch of the peninsula has been utilised for blocks of expensive flats and luxury style houses, many with gardens reaching down to the sandy shore.

Amongst the early dwellings was a row of coastguard cottages. Hugh Insley Fox, head of the leading south coast estate agents, Fox and Sons, bought one of these for £850 in 1934. I would not care to estimate its value today. In fact the whole of Sandbanks, now worth millions was once offered for sale by the Guest family who owned it, for £200 and there were no takers.

This sandy peninsula connected to the mainland by an isthmian road and sandy beach, which give properties along it views of the harbour on one side and the bay on the other, is the home of the Royal Motor Yacht Club. One of the leading powerboat clubs in the world, which has the Duke of Edinburgh as its Admiral. The RMYC today is very friendly, but at one time it was basically for the aristocracy. On the pages of its membership are the names of Lord Mountbatten, the Duke of Westminster, the Marquess of Milford Haven, The Marquess Camden, Earl Howe and Lord Iliffe. From the business world come household names: Worthington Brickwood and Dale, all brewers; Lyle, Palethorpe, Fox and Cadbury representing food and confectionery; W.L. Stephenson of Woolworth fame; Madame Schiaparelli, and Lois de Rothschild.

Col. Walter Bersey, the most autocratic of all the Commodores, reigned from 1933-48. The Colonel, who is reputed to have tried to stop a man who had almost drowned off the club jetty, from being brought into the clubhouse because he was not a member, was a stickler for protocol. He insisted on a ceremonial flag-raising each morning, and it was band leader Billy Cotton who once substituted the Ensign, and to the anger of Col. Bersey, the flag that broke out at the masthead was a Russian Red flag complete with Hammer and Sickle.

Another resident of Sandbanks with sporting connections was Mrs Louise Dingwall who trained her racehorses on the sands. She was one of the first women to hold a Trainers licence, and was still working when she was over ninety years old.

Sandbanks, because it is linked with the Studland shore by a chain ferry has become known as the Gateway to the Purbecks.

Sandford Orcas

County boundary changes are not new it would seem. Sandford Orcas, redolent of all that is idyllic in Dorset was in Somerset until 1896.

Like many other Dorset villages, its name has a ring of poetry.

This delightful place lies in hill country on the Dorset – Somerset border. Three streams rise in the parish and in Saxon times, the water was forded over a sandy bottom, from which the name Sandford derives.

In the century after the Battle of Hastings, the manor became the property of a Norman family known as Orescuilz, and that was not an easy name for the Saxon Dorset men to get their tongues around, so they called it Orcas.

The present Manor House, with a splendid gatehouse, goes back five hundred years to the Tudors and although built at the time Columbus was sailing west on his famous expedition it has changed little since. The church next door has an interesting 13th century font, shaped like an upturned Canterbury bell.

A strange wall monument of carved and painted alabaster shows a knight in armour, kneeling between his two wives and eleven children. Seven children kneel in black gowns and the others are in swaddling clothes of red and lying in a heap behind their mother. The knight, who rests below the memorial is William Knoyle who died a few years before Shakespeare.

The reading on the stone gives us more information on this strange tomb, dated 1607. It seems he married 'fillip, daughter of Robert Morgane by whom hee had yssve 4 children and bee dead'.

The knight's second wife was Grace Clavel, by whom he had three sons and four daughters, who survived him.

The pretty village is near Trent and is approached via a leafy lane from Poyntington.

Shapwick 🦀

There is no nautical reason why Shapwick, a Stourside village in the heart of Dorset's sheeplands, should have an Anchor Inn, or a legend surrounding a crab. This placid village only sees an abundance of water when the Stour in spate floods the meadows and the crossroads, making an island of the old stepped Preaching Cross.

The legend tells of a fishmonger from Poole travelling to Bere Regis (and that seems a long way round) who lost one of his finest crabs. It was found by a country clown who, horror struck, stamped on it because he thought it was the devil. He alerted the villagers who feared that with so many legs, the monster would travel at great speed. Village sage, shepherd Rowe, who had taken to his bed 6 years before, was wheeled in a barrow to the crab, and started to sweat in fear 'Tis a land monster, wheel me off', he cried. Eventually, the fishmonger returned and picked up the crustacean to the astonishment of all the villagers, who – to this day – hate the very name crab.

A publicity-minded publican at the Anchor has the poem of the legend, with an amusing picture strip, painted on the bar wall and at Mr Percy Tory's farm, a weather vane depicts the crab and men pushing the wheelbarrow.

Another Shapwick anachronism is the name Piccadilly Corner and no one knows why this famous London name crops up in a lonely Dorset lane.

A mile north-east of the village is Badbury Rings, ranking with Maiden Castle as one of the south's great earthworks.

Three ramparts, each about 40 feet high, separated by ditches, encircle the hill fort 330 feet high. A place with a view – it serves as a grandstand for the South Dorset Hunt's Point-to-Point meetings.

The farmer who planted the magnificent avenue of trees, which line about 2 miles of the Wimborne to Blandford road, beneath the Rings, is supposed to have set one for each day of the year. He could not count very well – there are over 365 on one side of the road but, in summer when the leaves are thick, and the sun illuminates thousands of love-pledges carved into the trunks of the ancient trees, it is one of Dorset's most beautiful rides.

Shillingstone

I believe many of the strange and amusing country games attributed to be-smocked country dwellers are instigated by 'townies' acting out their own rural fantasies, because they are jealous of the countryman's existence, free from the pressures and strains of city life.

Accepting that I may be mistaken, such a game – Dwyle Flonking – held its championship at Shillingstone in 1972. I am told that it is a game of Norfolk origin. Basically, teams of be-smocked contestants face each other, and a character stands between them with two chamber pots full of beer. As the teams move around him, he dunks a flannel into one of the pots and throws it at team members. Points are scored according to which area he hits and, if he misses, he has to drink the contents of the other pot.

Shillingstone, which derives its name from 'Schellings Town', because it belonged to Norman times to the Eschelling family, once had the tallest maypole in Dorset – 86 feet high. Continuous road widening, necessitated by growing traffic needs, reduced the green to not much more than a verge. Now no further encroachment can take place because the remaining land has been officially confirmed as a town or village green.

The village has lost two railways. One through the Beeching axe in 1965, and the other – a private line owned by the late Sir Thomas Salt. It ran around the grounds of his home at Shillingstone House. Sir Thomas, 3rd baronet, was a former High Sheriff of Dorset.

The village also possesses a graceful cross at its centre. A delicate Gothic pinnacle against a backdrop of the simple thatch of Dorset.

In the First World War, Shillingstone earned the title of 'England's Bravest Village'. His Majesty King George V was 'gratified to learn how splendidly the people of Shillingstone had responded to the call to the colours.' When the war was only six months old, the village of 563 men, women and children, had enlisted a record 90 men.

Shitterton 🐚

More sensitive Dorset folk, embarrassed by villages prefixed Piddle, changed the more prominent main road places to Puddle, but although the hamlet of Shitterton, near Bere Regis, for a long while changed its main road nameplate to Sitterton, I now see the village is once again proudly marked with its true name. Poor Arthur Mee, who changed all the Piddles to Puddles, completely ignored Shitterton and missed recording one of the loveliest squares of thatched cottages in the county.

Shroton 🐚

When Cromwell sent 50 dragoons to drag the Clubmen from Hambledon Hill in 1645, it was probably as comic a battle as the re-enactment by villagers carried out when Princess Marie Louise visited Shroton in 1951.

Briefly, if you are not a student of history, the Clubmen were countryfolk, often generalled by clergy, who had grown weary of the battles between Cavaliers and Roundheads, which damaged their lands and ruined the crops. Few of them knew the merits of the

SHROTON   JOHN BAKER

quarrel between King and Parliament but, armed with clubs, pitch-forks and scythe blades, they took issue with both sides. Their only uniform was a white cockcade. They took a battering wherever they defended their land and, finally, some of them became entrenched on Hambledon Hill, led by the Rev. Bravel of Compton Abbas.

Cromwell's dragoons overcame them and chased 300 of them down the slopes to be locked up in Shroton church. It is said that some escaped by sliding down the hill on their bottoms, amongst them 4 clergy. The Clubmen were released next day and went home, having had enough of battle.

Later, a more modern army mustered on the Hill under General Wolfe and used it as a training ground for their assault on Quebec.

Shroton, in a lane which loops off the main Blandford to Shaftes-bury road, has changed little and, sitting in the church, you can imagine the 300 Clubmen cursing and quarrelling in the pews through the long summer night nearly 350 years ago.

The church used to be reflected in a weedy pond – to the delight of photographs and artists – but, on my last visit, it had dried up.

Shroton celebrated the 700th anniversary of its Charter in 1961 but the great fairs, which included amusements and horse and pony sales, ended before the First World War. Both Thomas Hardy and William Barnes remember them.

128

Hardy saw a woman 'beheaded' in a sideshow, but Barnes remembers the Fair days with his usual delight, because the dialect poet turned his back on all that was distasteful and ugly. Here is part of his long poem which I have changed into plain language.

'We saw the dancers in a show
Dance up and down, and to and fro,
Upon a rope with chalky soles,
So light as magpies up on poles
And tumblers, with their streaks and spots,
That all but tied theirselves in knots.
And then a conjurer burned off
Poll's handkerchief so blacks a snoff, (snuff)
And hit it with a single blow,
Right back again so white as snow.
And after that, he fried a fat
Great cake inside of my new hat;
And yet, for all he did him brown,
He did not even zweal the crown.'

Sixpenny Handley

The first half-dozen times I drove uphill through Sixpenny Handley and on to the Cranborne Chase proper, I saw not a living soul, which led me to regard it as something in the nature of *Brigadoon* or an inland *Marie Celeste*.

Even though I have since encountered plenty of local inhabitants, the thought has remained, aided and abetted by history.

This was one of the homes of the dreaded Isaac Gulliver whose smuggling operations spread from Poole to Lyme Regis. He married the daughter of a local landlord and made the pub one of his head-quarters.

Those who think that smuggling has, of necessity, to be carried on somewhere near the sea, might note that Sixpenny Handley is around 30 miles inland, which is a long way to travel, loaded and under cover of darkness. Gulliver, though he had a liking for spirits and lace, might well have had another string to his bow – an enterprise founded on the availability of deer on the Chase ... and a tomb adjoining the local church where 'hot' vension could be stored for the duration of the hue and cry.

In 1892, the village suffered a devastating fire, in which 'nearly 200 people were rendered homeless and destitute.' It surprised me to learn there were that many villagers – they must have lived about 20 to the house – but something about the tragedy caught the public imagination because people rallied around in a way for which Oxfam have been praying ever since, and it was said that you could always tell a Sixpenny Handley man for some time afterwards because he usually wore two if not three waistcoats.

A great deal of money was collected and when all claims were met, there remained at least £1,000. But so much squabbling arose over how this large (in those days) sum was to be spent that it was put into Chancery and remains there, as far as I know, to this day.

But the love of money has nothing to do with the name of the village, which is derived from the two medieval hundreds of Saxpena and Hanlege ('Saxon hilltop' and 'high clearing').

Spetisbury 🐦

The traveller, racing north to Blandford, is apt to take Spetisbury for granted – anther very long village with a narrowing street which impedes his journey.

One of Spetisbury's little inns bore a colourful sign depicting a steam train. That, however, is now a memory because the train, which dropped generations of Spetisbury folk at their own halt right in the village centre, was axed by Dr. Beeching about two decades ago. The inn has now closed and the inn sign removed. An enormous petrol filling station nearby reminds us of today's travel needs.

If you do have time to stop, Spetisbury has one of those magnificent bridges which cross the winding Stour on its journey south. Built in the 15th century, it has nine arches.

Earthworks, known as Spetisbury Rings, were a stronghold long before the Romans came, and Roman and Briton lie side by side in graves dug after some forgotten battle.

The church chiefly built of flint has a beautiful pulpit from Stuart times. Once Spetisbury had an abundance of woodpeckers because it takes its name from speht – woodpecker, and byrig – a fort.

Stalbridge

I have a lingering memory of Stalbridge, beyond Sturminster Newton in the north of the county. When a young photographer, I had been assigned to cover a Christmas Market at Sturminster Newton, a festive social occasion. On my way home from my assignment, I have never forgotten gazing out of the train window in the darkness and seeing an aged porter holding an oil lamp aloft so that the eerie light illuminated his countenance. He was shouting 'Stalbridge, Stalbridge, this do be Stalbridge'.

It was quite a while before I discovered this attractive place in daylight, and learned that the world owed a great debt to a man who once lived there; Robert Boyle, the man who showed how air could be compressed and gave us the pneumatic tyre.

He inherited the old Elizabethan house which stood at Stalbridge, but if fate had triumphed he would never have made his discoveries, because he was not only nearly drowned whilst crossing a river on horseback, but narrowly escaped death when a ceiling collapsed on him.

He went to Eton at eight years of age, and it was soon obvious that he was to become a genius. His further pursuit of knowledge led him abroad.

He returned and although still a young man became an associate of the country's leading scientists. Nothing escaped his interest and he delved into physics, anatomy, religion and philosophy. But it was his experiments at Stalbridge into the laws of pneumatics by which we remember him most, improving the air pump and showing how there were countless uses for his compressed air.

Sadly the house at Stalbridge Park is no more, only the gate piers remain, surmounted by heraldic beasts. It was demolished in 1822 and prints of the old house which have survived show a house with Jacobean motifs of an idiosyncratic cast. Some of the park wall also remains.

Stalbridge also possesses a rare 30 foot high Market Cross in yellow Ham stone. It escaped the wrath of the Civil Wars and unlike so many others, a useless stump in a base, this one has the distinction of never having been altered or restored. Although slightly eroded it must have been a splendid piece when it was built in the late 15th century.

131

Standing in the High Street, it has a three stepped octagonal base supporting the pedestal carved with the images of biblical figures. Its position is very vulnerable from passing traffic, and villagers fear that a lorry speeding through may demolish it.

In the days when it had town status it was called Staplebridge, and Leland described it as 'a praty uplandishe towne of one streate neately well buildyd'. But Treves was not so impressed when he came, commenting on a row of semi-detached villas worthy of the suburbs of Hull, its leaning to slate, iron railings and much bill-posting,' but he loved the cross, 'tanned by the sun'.

Some amusing names on gravestones in the churchyard of St Mary might have inspired Dickens. Temperance Collins, Ismond Plainewit, and Matthew Foole all died in the 17th century.

Stapehill

The main road from Ringwood to Wimborne separates two vastly different ways of life at Stapehill.

The Old Thatch, with brightly flowered garden, is an inn of quality with good ale and excellent food served in cosy bars. There is carefree laughter in this oasis for pleasure seekers who need a change from crowded Dorset seasides. But, across the road, a field away is a Cistercian nunnery, a gaunt brick building where, in seclusion, live an order of nuns who have given their lives to contemplation and penance. They ignore the outside world, observe Greenwich Mean Time all the year round and rise before daylight each day. After Tierce, the Mother Superior details the tasks for the day. They include housework and the running of a 25 acre farm. The nuns retire to bed at 7 p.m. in the winter and 8 p.m. during the summer.

My one and only visit to this very private community was in 1937. Mrs Myldrede Humble-Smith, a local author, contributed a story to the *Evening Echo* Bournemouth on life in the nunnery, and arranged with the Abbess for me to be hidden within the grounds to photograph the nuns as they filed out to work in the hayfields. Wearing picturesque straw headgear, which concealed their faces unless viewed head on, they turned the hay and I clicked merrily away taking pictures, until one of their number spotted me and, as she approached pitchfork in hand, I beat a hasty retreat and vowed never to return.

Steeple, with Creech and Church Knowle

Glole, Stipple, and Griz. It sounds like a firm of solicitors in a Dickens novel, but these were the Domesday Book names for Church Knole, Steeple and Creech. Later Steeple and the now dead village of Tyneham were united.

Steeple is a little hamlet with a delightful manor house, a farm and a church with a strange claim to fame. Long before the American flag was thought of, the Stars and Stripes were carved into the church wall. The Lawrences, who were the squires of Steeple were allied with the ancestors of George Washington.

It appears that the two families, both from the Duchy of Lancaster intermarried in the 14th century. In 1540 the Lawrences came to Steeple, whilst a descendant of the Washingtons settled in Virginia and became the great grandfather of George Washington, the first President of the USA.

It is thought that the American flag, often seen in the church today, to the delight of American visitors, was derived from the design of the Lawrence Coat of Arms.

A rector in 1682 aptly named Samuel Bolde, declared in a sermon that 'everybody had a right to their own beliefs'. It angered King James II so much that Bolde was imprisoned.

The church has a unique barrel organ, the tune being picked out by pins and staples on a drum which when revolving strikes reeds of different tuning.

The Manor House was amongst several homes viewed as a possible place for retirement for Sir Anthony Eden in the 1950s but the idea was probably dropped because of the persistent noise of gunfire from the Lulworth ranges.

From Steeple climb up a rolling Dorset Down, nearly 700 feet high and a descent the other side brings the visitor into Creech and the sight of the grand home of the Bonds. The Bonds of Bond Street who took over in 1691 hold it to this day. It was Thomas Bond who in Stuart times laid out the famous London Street over fields of swamp and refuse tips.

Church Knowle is the 'village on a hillock', the burial place of ancient Britons. The Saxons named it cnoll – a hillock. In Domesday the village was called Chenolle. Today we are left with an attractive village in the Purbeck style with a 13th century church, ancient manor house and an inn, very traditional and cosy. The east window of the church depicts Jesus walking on the water and Peter sinking.

Stoke Abbot

A beautiful village nestling along deep lanes in an amphitheatre of hills with several thatched houses, Stoke Abbot has escaped the attention of guidebooks probably because it is not near any main road. The predominant traffic is farm vehicles. Straggling roads have spread haphazardly out from the Norman church and cottages of mellow Ham Hill limestone with mullioned windows which catch and hold the quiet sun.

It was a former rector, William Crowe, who loved this place so much that he wrote a poem about Lewesdon Hill, one of the heights above the village, and one of the highest in the county from the tree-clad slopes he mused:

'Above the noisy stir of yonder field
Uplifted on this height I feel the mind
Expand itself in wider liberty.'

Wordsworth thought it was an admirable poem.

Stourpaine

Where the little river Ewerne meets the Stour, beneath the great hill called Hod, is Stourpaine. The main Shaftesbury road divides two communities – a modern council estate on one side, and cob and thatched cottages around a church with battlements atop its 500 year old tower on the other.

Stourpaine boasts one unusual piece of architecture – Hod Cottage, with an ancient upstairs window from which generations of village maidens have gossiped with passers-by for 400 years. But its main attraction is the hill, which has traces of occupations by Ancient Britons and Romans. Tools, pottery, fragments of harness

134

and coins bearing the names of several Emperors, have been found on the hilltop.

An annual Steam Rally at Stourpaine Bushes introduces school-children from all over Dorset to the well-loved fairground and farmyard steam engines, which were popular earlier in this century.

STUDLAND (OLD HARRY ROCKS)   JOHN BAKER

Studland

Quaint Studland, cossetted amongst trees, hides itself from both main road and sea yet it has much beauty and interest. The traveller, having fortified himself at the Bankes Arms, can pass through a gate to embark on one of Dorset's loveliest walks, along the cliff edge to the chalk sentinel of the Purbecks, Old Harry Rock. Lonely now that time and the elements have robbed him of his 'wife', but a pleasant place to sit and ponder.

Before the tractor came, fine horses dragging farm equipment made their turn almost on the cliff edge, before taking the strain to surmount the slopes of Ballard Down.

Old Harry has witnessed a long history of shipwrecks and, at his feet, Coxswain William Brown was washed overboard and drowned from the Swanage lifeboat, *William Erle II,* on her maiden call in 1895. The great rock has faced the Channel gales for centuries, so it is natural that the stocky and very old church is dedicated to the patron saint of sailors, but it has changed little since the

Normans built it 800 years ago. The tower is squat and unfinished as the builders left it, waiting for foundations to settle. Some of its walls are reddened with lichen and the yews in the churchyard are very old. The sloping churchyard offers a wondrous view of the cliffs to Ballard Down.

On two sides of a tombstone the love story of a warrior whose name you may not find in the history books is revealed.

Sgt. William Lawrence, of the 40th Regiment of Foot, saw a decade of active service mostly against the French, and lost his heart to a French woman whom he married and brought home to Studland. In 1805, he was in South America fighting Spaniards; in the Peninsular Wars he fought in most of Wellington's battles. A volunteer for the storming of Badajos, he was severely wounded but recovered to fight again at Waterloo. It was on the subsequent march to Paris that he fell in love with Clotilde Clairet at Germain-en-Laye. They settled in Studland and kept an inn and when he died 54 years after Waterloo, volunteers fired a volley over his grave.

The landings on French soil in the Second World War were rehearsed on the lovely sandy beaches of Studland. It was a training ground for invasion forces.

The Agglestone, situated on the heathland 1 mile north-east, is 17 feet high and weighs about 400 tons, but how it was placed on its mound is a mystery. I would discount the local belief that it landed there when the Devil was throwing stones at Old Harry from the Isle of Wight.

Sturminster Marshall

Turn off from the nave-like line of trees which forms the avenue at Badbury Rings and cross the magnificent medieval eight-arched bridge spanning the Stour, and enter Sturminster Marshall.

Around a corner into the village, the traveller may be surprised by a giant, colourful old woman's shoe, and a mousetrap large enough to catch a deer, in the garden of a bungalow. These are glass fibre creations of the owner of Ramblers Roost, next to a line of cottages destroyed by fire in the 1970s, and lovingly rebuilt in their original external style.

A much earlier fire had more tragic consequences. John Truelove, a wealthy London surgeon who retired to the Stourside village, took

136

to riotous living and lost his fortune. In 1724, anticipating a visit from the Sheriff's officer, he filled his cottage with furze and, before an amazed crowd, set light to the house and appearing at his bedroom window, shot himself and fell back into the flames.

The re-fashioned church in this proud village stands on Norman foundations and new dwellings built to enlarge its population around a picturesque green, are in keeping with older parts of the village.

STURMINSTER NEWTON   JOHN BAKER

Sturminster Newton

Residents may not take it kindly if I include Sturminster Newton amongst the villages of Dorset, but this lovely Minster town, cut in two by the gently flowing Stour, embodies all the ingredients of a true village and has maintained its character.

The motorist, hurrying toward Sherborne only sees Newton with its picturesque cottages, but wander over the ancient bridge which still bears a notice threatening deportation if you cause damage, and come to a Town Planner's nightmare. No two houses alike or in line, built in brick, stone, thatch, whitened cob and some exposed Tudor style timbering. In the Square are two friendly inns, but at various times builders have set houses in the centre of the Square splitting it into a conglomoration of narrow roads, which get choked by the great vehicles which bring the animals to market.

On a sunny morning it is full of old world charm. Gentlemen move off the narrow pavements (some only 18 inches wide) to let you pass, and doff their hats to ladies, receiving a smile in return.

Little shops hide behind 19th century facades and loud ringing bells announce the arrival of customers. This is a corner of rural England unchanged in two hundred years.

137

I remember coming to Sturminster on a snowy Christmas Eve, and in the cosy bar of the White Hart enjoyed the entertainment as butcher, baker and blacksmith dropped in to do their party pieces. Outside under snow-laden eaves, a choir of children grouped around the old Cross steps and sang carols as children did when the dialect poet William Barnes went to school here, more than 150 years before.

Even today farmers meet together with friends and spend winter evenings reading Parson Barnes's soothing verse.

> 'We Do'set, though we mid be hwomely,
> Be'ntf asheamed to own our pleace;
> An we've some women not uncomely;
> nor asheamed to show their feace.'

It was not so peaceful at Sturminster in the days of Barnes. Then it was an important town with factories producing buttons, candles and metal goods. Workers often indulged in brutal drunken fights and in the Square public floggings took place.

On the other side of the bridge is a mound on which a Saxon castle once stood, overlooking the Town Mill, still working for visitors to see.

Although a very ancient place, it is not the distant past which put Sturminster into the history books, but a contemporary event which brought sadness and resentment to its people.

Sturminster has an important cattle market and in 1935 whilst the market was in progress, foot and mouth disease was discovered at nearby Shroton. The Ministry of Agriculture ordered all animals to be confined to the market and 2000 sheep, cattle and pigs were shot and their carcases burned in a massive grave of 15,000 sq. yds. It caused consternation and grief amongst the farming folk and is remembered to this day.

The traveller Leland once described Sturminster as 'no great thing', but today it stands as a peaceful monument to a way of life long since forgotten now that progress has led us into an age governed by the computer, and journeys that lead us to the moon and beyond.

Sutton Poyntz

This once pretty hamlet, the 'Overcombe' of Hardy's novel *The Trumpet Major*, has been overtidied. Not for one moment would I deny residents the tiled roof comfort of the cottages by the pond, but I remember when they were overladen with thick thatch, reflected in the water, where the ducks swam between overladen branches of green willow drooping into the pond. It is, however, a village looked after by those who live here, and quaint corners are kept beautiful with floral displays. The Weymouth Waterworks does not add to the charm.

Many visitors come this way to climb up to the Iron Age fort of Chalbury, half a mile west, but the walk east across fields to the famous White Horse, carved into the chalk hill, is a fond memory of my boyhood. The 250 foot high and 300 foot wide carving of King George III astride his horse is visible from Weymouth and Portland – a feature being the enormous tail, as wide as a street.

As a child, I would sit on the King's head and muse on the legendary story of the man who executed the carving throwing himself over the cliffs to death, when he realised that he had portrayed His Majesty leaving town. Simple truth is that it was cut in 1807 to the order of one John Ranier, under the supervision of a Mr. Wood, a local bookseller, and it is possible that he was purposely portrayed going east to visit his friend Sir Thomas Weld at Lulworth.

Swyre & Puncknowle

A fishmonger who hailed from Scotland to sell his catches to the ancient abbeys, and a local farmer are remembered in plaques on the walls of the little church at Swyre, just off the coast near Bridport.

John Russell, the farmer whose farmhouse was nearby, was called to assist a Spanish princess wrecked off Weymouth because of his knowledge of languages. He went with her to the King in London and was accepted at Court by Henry VII. In the reign of Henry VIII he became Lord Russell, founder of the fortunes of the House of Bedford.

Fishmonger, James Napier, headed another famous family founded in the reign of Henry VII.

Puncknowle, a mile to the north, has in its church memorials to generations of the Napier family. The church has a tower constructed in three storeys and is 12th century, reconstructed in the 17th century.

Amongst the elaborate Napier memorials, is the helmet which once carried the Napier crest which, with the spurs and gauntlets, were stolen in 1975.

According to the Domesday Book, prior to the Conquest, the manor was in the hands of a Saxon named Alward. After the Conquest in 1066, it came into the hands of 'Hugh, Son of Grip', and before the end of the 15th century, eight families owned the area including the Napiers who, in 1710, sold it to William Clutterbuck, a Devon sea captain. It now belongs to the Bridgemans Estates.

Puncknowle is perhaps better known as the home of the man whose name sends shudders down the backs of servicemen and, come to think of it, civilians too ... Colonel Shrapnel, who invented the devastating shell which bears his name and has been one of the most dreaded weapons of soldiers and terrorists.

Sydling St. Nicholas

Here is a corner of old England at its basic best. An unpretentious village straggling along the little Sydling Water, with tiny connecting bridges, to the ancient cottages which line the banks.

In summer the visitor may wander in peace to view walls covered in roses and clematis and pause for a while at the old Ham Stone Cross before entering the church through a gate alongside the Manor House. Built in the 1400s and rebuilt in the 18th century, it has a fireplace inside the porch where, at one time, villagers sat to hold parish meetings. The font is over 1000 years old, thought to have been carved from an ancient Roman capital. The clock, one of the oldest in England and dated 1593, is faceless but strikes the hours. Amongst the memorials is one for a young apprentice glazier, 15-year old John Webber, ordered by his employer to help with contraband, and shot by coastguard men and killed. There are yew trees said to be over 1000 years old.

The school started in 1797, was in use until 1966, and is now a dwelling. The 1793 bakery and old brewery are protected buildings, and, yes, Sydling has a blacksmith and a spreading chestnut tree.

Beneath the surrounding hills terraced traces of the old Celtic linchet cultivation system are visible, and it is to the peace of Sydling that salmon come home to spawn after a long and hazardous upstream journey from Poole. If I were a salmon, I would find a quiet pool somewhere along this long journey.

Symondsbury ⚜

There is much thatch in this little west Dorset village, predominantly built of yellow sandstone dwellings, because it is noted for its thatching craftsmen.

Like many other outposts of the county, it has suffered little change in the 20th century, but boasts of having electric light seven years before the town of Bridport. Major Sir Philip Colfox formed the Symondsbury Electric Light Company to illuminate the village, and a local blacksmith made the iron-work fittings.

The church is 14th century, on the site of an earlier building, and the organ was given in memory of the Sweet brothers, Captain Len, who was killed in 1916, and the Rev. George – drowned whilst punting on his honeymoon.

This is cider making country and the rural art was revived when gamekeeper Jack Cook died in the 1970s and left his cider-making press to the villagers. Sir John Colfox helped in its restoration and the delicious juice is now regularly made. In 1981 the villagers became very angry over the felling of an 80ft. oak tree.

The Tarrants – Gunville, Monkton, Launceston, Rawston, Rushton, Hinton, Keyneston, & Crawford ⚜

For a thousand years the little river Tarrant has flooded meadows and villages along its short course. That is why it was first called Terente (trespasser), and a journey along the 8 miles of quiet road from Gunville, its source, to Crawford where it empties into the Stour, is rewarded by the discovery of some interesting and lovely places.

Of the 8 villages and hamlets, Rushton has stolen the limelight because the Downs above it became the site of a wartime airfield which not only played a major role in the 1939-45 conflict, but later became the base for early experiments carried out by Sir Alan Cobhams's Flight Refuelling Company. This method of refuelling aircraft in mid-air proved its worth during the Falklands crisis of 1982. Many famous types of aircraft have soared up over the Dorset fields. Halifax bombers towed Horsa gliders over the sullen Badbury rings on their way to Arnhem, and little Lysanders, engaged in cloak and dagger activities, carried agents out over the Dorset coast in moonlight to sneak into France. During the experiments in refuelling, Lancasters and Meteors shattered the serenity of the Stour valley. The Martens, landowners from Crichel, won their battle for the return of the land to agriculture and now there is silence because tractors have torn the runways asunder, and only an occasional vapour trail offers defiance, almost like a silent protest.

Rushton is at peace and the traveller crosses the Tarrant to see the ancient church dating back to the 12th century, shaped like a cross with all four arms of equal length.

Gunville is at the river's source but the important looking if decaying, entrance to Eastbury Hall almost overbears the mansion, which can be glimpsed at the top of the park. It has but a single wing, but it was not always so. Two hundred years ago a dandy, George Bubb Dodington, son of a Weymouth apothecary, built the mansion on the lines of Blenheim Palace. He had been left a fortune and spent £140,000 on its construction. Most of it was pulled down after his death because it could not be maintained. As Lord Melcombe, he died young and it is said that he slept in a bed canopied with peacock feathers.

The church has a memorial to Thomas Wedgwood, son of the famous Josiah, who died in the year of Trafalgar. He contributed to early experiments in photography and eventually built a basic camera, but he was denied a major role in the birth of this popular art because he died before discovering a means of fixing his images to make them permanent.

Downstream, we reach Tarrant Hinton, spoiled because it suffers the fast road from Salisbury to Blandford, but the church is secreted at the end of a lane of great charm. During the Great War, men of the Naval Division trained here before going to Gallipoli, where most of them perished.

Monkton and Launceston cluster together where the lanes twist, and are separated by a little 3 arched bridge and a gurgling water splash.

Monkton is a proud village which, as my old grandmother would say, 'keeps itself to itself'. The people care for their village, keep well-trimmed thatched roofs and some have wishing wells in lovely flowered gardens. The village shop bears its name in Olde English lettering and, in the fields, well-groomed Jacobs rams constantly graze. The villagers care for their own, and pride of place outside the excellent inn, is taken by an 8ft. Memorial to four sons of Launceston and Monkton who gave their lives in the 1914-18 war.

The river winds down the valley to Rawston, now mainly a farmstead, where a miniature water wheel, 18 ins. across housed in a little brick building 6 ft. square, stands beside a gentle waterfall, and comes to Keyneston.

Speeding traffic through Keyneston has led it to be described as having 'the fastest High Street in the West'. Whether you approach from the north, passing beautiful cottages clinging to the hillside, or from the south leaving the long avenue of trees behind, the route is sharply downhill with clear vision both ways, but the valley is the village centre – little changed in a hundred years. The crossroads has its shops on one corner, the school building on another, and an inn – swinging the rare sign of the True Lovers Knot. It commemorates the lovers symbol, a complicated double knot with interlacing bows on each side and two ends. Why it is so is a mystery. A Norman, William de Cahagnes, ruled the Saxons in the Tarrant valley and, from Tarente Kahaines, the village gets its new name.

The Tarrant ends its journey at Crawford and although the village is dominated by the Stour and its nine-arched bridge, it takes its name from the smaller river. Crow Ford the Saxons called it, an interesting name because just across the Stour is Spetisbury, named after another bird, the woodpecker.

Tincleton

Tincleton was recorded in the Domesday Book and today the village serves as an alternative route for those who journey down the road to see Hardy's cottage at Higher Bockhampton.

Its centre piece is a mansion built on the village slopes, called Clyffe House.

The rebellious Clement Walker was born at Tincleton. He was expelled from Parliament by 'Pride's Purge' in 1648 because of his outspoken criticism of Cromwell and the army. He was imprisoned in the Tower where he died. Amongst many books he wrote was *High Court of Justice or Cromwell's New Slaughter House.*

Tollard Royal

A peaceful inland village, which is actually in Wiltshire but I have included it in this book because it is much loved by Dorset people as a beautiful spot really very close to the border! It is set in a narrow, thickly wooded valley and is approached from the Cranborne direction (B3078) via a long avenue of beeches. The gentle green slopes which rise away from the road on all sides swarm with sheep and their spring-heeled offspring. The pastureland is generously supplied with tumps from which Larry and his brothers and sisters and cousins can launch forth in ructions that have taken them into vernal folklore, and given mint sauce a bad name.

Tollard was made 'royal' by the presence of a hunting lodge for King John, who used to meet his hunt companions about a mile above the village under the Larmer Tree (a wych elm), which finally blew down in 1894 and was replaced by an oak. The Larmer Tree memory lives on, however, with annual pageants at the home of Michael Pitt-Rivers which raise funds for the Friends of the Salisbury Museum.

The Larmer Gardens are unique. Grouped around a field are Eastern temples, statues and an open air theatre, the stage set in a shell-shaped proscenium.

Cecil Beaton rented an all-but-stately home near Ashmore during the late 1920s and the 1930s and most weekends were made flamboyant and raucous by the presence of his guests.

Their forays into the village to examine the rustics rather in the style of Sunday afternoon coach-trips to Bethlehem Asylum – not 'slumming', quite; perhaps 'hovelling' would be a better word – led them to dismiss the Tollard Royalists as rather miserable types with not much imagination.

What the gentle, sheltered peasantry made of the Beaton crowd is not on record.

Toller Fratrum

Toller Fratrum stands on a hillside overlooking the Hooke as it prepares to meet the larger river Frome. It was once the Toller of the Brothers, where the Knights Hospitallers had their storehouses. A long thatched building on which there is a carving of a man eating a loaf is believed to have been their refectory.

The Manor House, built by Royalist Sir Thomas Fulford, is one of Dorset's loveliest houses – an excellent specimen of the domestic architecture of the 17th century. The grey masonry is weathered and bronzed by age, and twisted stone chimneys overshadow pinnacles formed into heraldic beasts.

The church is unique, dedicated to Basil the Great who is honoured as one of the greatest saints in the Churches of the East, and only three in the whole of England are dedicated to him.

Toller Porcorum

It is inappropriate that the sweet-sounding name of Toller Porcorum on the banks of the River Hooke only tells us that it is the 'valley of the pigs'. Toller meaning a stream in a valley. Formerly it was named Swynestolre or Hogstolre, the toller of the pigs.

Once kings hunted wild boar here, but now deer, foxes, badgers and hares swarm over the land which has evidence of being lived on since prehistoric times.

The church is old, but not as old as its font; that is part of a Roman altar – shaped before this country was England.

West of the village is Eggardon Hill, supporting an Iron Age fort, and the Romans are believed to have been here in 43 AD. The church is dedicated to St. Andrew and St. Peter and not only are there records dating back to 1235, but it was served by priests hundreds of years before. The village school was founded in 1772.

Toller Porcorum is one of those Dorset villages fighting to stop population growth and new estates. In 1983 planners wanted to build 15 terraced cottages. Permission was refused.

The school which finally closed its doors in 1980 bears the name of Julia Harrison on its registers. The daughter of Rev. John Harrison, a former vicar, Julia shook off her village girl image and grew up to become Fiona Richmond, controversial author and actress.

Tolpuddle

Violence on picket lines and bloody battles between striking workers and police would seem to have little in common with a little village green in Dorset, yet beneath a giant sycamore at Tolpuddle six farm labourers banded together in 1831 and made a pact which was the beginning of Trade Unionism in England.

There was no violence, they were good men and had deep Christian beliefs, but they decided to ask for 3 extra shillings a week to 'save their families from starvation and utter degradation'.

A judge at Dorchester sent George Loveless and his companions to a penal colony in Australia for 7 years, 'not for anything they had

146

done, or intended to do, but as an example to others'. They were later pardoned.

The Tolpuddle Martyrs contributed a proud chapter in the history of Trade Unionism and in 1934 the T.U.C. erected six memorial cottages in the village. Once a year, leading Socialist politicians, under colourful banners, march past the Green where now a commemorative seat and shelter have been erected.

In 1936, at a memorial arch outside the Methodist Chapel, David Lloyd George laid a wreath — in fact, the famous former Prime Minister laid it several times until each press cameraman was satisfied. Just before the Second World War the famous actress, Dame Sybil Thorndike, and her husband, Lewis Casson, who were appearing in play called 'The Six Men of Dorset', came and enacted some of the scenes around the Martyr's Tree.

Hard to believe that this lovely village of thatch, with its meadows watered by the gentle river Piddle, and a church with Norman remains, is one of the most famous villages in the world.

Trent

The amusing and prolonged saga of the future Charles II's flight after the battle of Worcester ended at Trent, where he had been hiding at Col. Francis Wyndham's manor house.

The famous battle had been fought on September 3, a date to be remembered in history. On that same date 288 years later, Britain declared war on Germany.

Charles arrived at Trent, which has changed little and is still a beautiful village of stone dwellings and rich orchards, disguised as the servant of Jane Lane.

The Prince's hiding place off Lady Wyndham's room is still preserved. Charles became petulant when church bells disturbed him, and even more angry when he was told that the villagers had rung them because, mistakenly, they thought he had been captured.

On September 22 he set out for Charmouth and a promised boat which would take him to France. The party consisted of Col. Wyndham, Lord Wilmot, Juliana Coningsby and the poor Prince in his now established role of lady's servant. The elopement of Wilmot and Juliana was their cover story, should they be stopped. The boat did not arrive and they returned to Trent, having narrow escapes from capture at Bridport and Broadwindsor.

147

Charles and Wilmot finally left Dorset in early October and the Prince made flight from English soil on a coal boat at Shoreham. Incidentally, the collier was bound for Poole and made a detour to drop the Prince in France.

Both captain and boat were honoured for their service. The old collier was cleaned up and became a Royal Yacht with her captain in charge.

Trent's church, with a lofty 14th century tower and spire, is the resting place of not only the Wyndhams, but Field Marshal Lord Rawlinson, one of our Commanders in the First World War.

In more recent days, Trent boasts of having an Archbishop of Canterbury as its rector. Lord Fisher of Lambeth retired to the village in the 1960s.

Tyneham 🍃

Tyneham was once a pleasing and proud hamlet in a fertile valley at the foot of one of the highest hills in the Purbeck Range. An Elizabethan Mansion, a handful of grey cottages, a fine church, and a school was home to a small rural community, near the coast at Worbarrow.

When the War Office chose to make it the centre of a Tank Firing Range at the beginning of the 1939-45 war it was evacuated and slowly decayed.

Creeping brambles and colourful wild flowers cloaked the scars of shellfire for many years after the end of the War, and now enthusiasts have cleared the site and tidied up the ruins to create a memorial to a village sacrificed to the needs of war. The schoolhouse has been restored to form a museum and meeting hall.

No one will live at Tyneham again and it can only be visited when the guns are silent.

A few weeks before it was evacuated in 1942 the Post Office had installed a grand new telephone kiosk for the villagers, decorated in the then traditional cream concrete style with the familiar ornate cupola roof.

It still remains, sealed, brightly repainted, and reminiscent of a Dr Who Time Capsule which has just arrived in a dead village.

TYNEHAM   JOHN BAKER

Upton

Upton, now another of the residential dormitories for the rapidly expanding port of Poole is built around a crossroads with a complex roundabout, where the Blandford to Hamworthy road crosses the main Poole to Dorchester road. In the fringe of the village is a house that, although not large, is one of the most interesting in Dorset. After a long history, closely connected with Poole, it has rightly come into the hands of local people who, with loving care, run it as a public place.

Upton House is set on a knoll, forty five feet above sea level overlooking Poole harbour, and a corridor of lawns free of trees gives a clear view of the harbour and little Pergins Island from Upton's terraces. It is a solid grey slate roofed house, echoing the elegance of late 18th and 19th century Britain.

The Upton Estate, standing beside an old Roman road, came into the hands of William Spurrier, a wealthy merchant who had amassed a fortune from the trade between Poole and Newfoundland in the mid-18th century. When he died, the estate passed to his son Christopher, one time M.P. for Bridport. It was he who built the present house in about 1818, in the Italian style, sparing no expense, and a few years later added the west wing. He cunningly enlarged his frontal parkland by diverting the Poole to Weymouth road.

In 1828 the house was sold to Edward Tichbourne-Doughty, whose nephew Roger stayed there, and the estate formed part of the law suit and scandal which shocked the Victorians, relating to the Tichbourne claimants; for it was after Roger Tichbourne disappeared, having been refused permission to marry his cousin, that Arthur Orton, an Australian, pursued his 'rights'. His claim was not established and it was castigated as 'the most daring and sustained imposture that ever afforded the measure of the possible wickedness of man'.

Between 1834 and 1853 Sir Edward, as he had become, added the east wing and chapel in the Cottage style of architecture.

It has been suggested that the house was the inspiration for Wyndaway House in Thomas Hardy's novel *The Hand of Ethelberta*.

In 1901, William Llewellin, who became High Sheriff of Dorset in 1919, bought the house and in 1936 planted an avenue of forty eight lime trees to commemorate the accession of King Edward VIII to the Throne. The trees failed, perhaps in sympathy with the King's abdication.

One of his sons was to become Lord Llewellin, First Governor General of the Rhodesias and Nyasaland. His daughter, Mary, was Poole's first ever Lady Mayor in 1951.

The Llewellin family lived at Upton House until 1957, when it was given to Poole Council with covenants in favour of the National Trust, and from 1961 to 1969 the house was occupied by Carol of Hohenzollern, Prince of Roumania.

The listed house is of special architectural interest because of its unusual curving colonnaded screens on either side of the main block. Inside, the central hall is paved with black marble and Portland stone. The hall rises the full height of the building, and is lit by a domed lantern.

150

In one of the ground floor rooms, there is a chimney piece of Italian statuary marble which was originally carved for a palace of the Emperor Napoleon I. Ceilings are in Adam style plaster work.

It might have become a zoo in the 1950s. Gerald Durrell cast his eyes over Uptons' acres, but soon after, established his zoo on Jersey.

1976 was a proud year for Poole people. A charity was formed known as the Friends of Upton Country Park. Their aim was to assist the Poole Council in the restoration of the house and grounds.

Through fund raising, they have provided facilities, such as a refreshment kiosk and picnic tables. A job creation scheme restored the brickwork of the walled garden and rebuilt the greenhouses. A fresh water lake has been created and is now stocked with ducks and geese. It is an ideal setting for the twice yearly Country Fayre.

The Friends have now started on the interior of the house, through a restoration appeal launched in 1981. The ground floor is already open to the public and staffed by voluntary stewards.

Nature trails with summer and winter routes are laid out, and as the shores of Upton are in the most northerly part of the harbour, the mud flats have become covered with rice grass, an ideal habitat for salt marsh birds.

However, it is a very simple corner of this lovely park which will probably remain in the memory. When the grounds were being cleared of undergrowth, in a secluded corner near the house, the gardeners found a pets' cemetery. Tombstones mark the last resting place of a dozen or more pets who lived at Upton over the years since 1882. The stones recall Rover, a collie who was born at Harwick in 1882 and died on the railway at Creekmoor in 1903. Pets are remembered back to the time of the Tichbournes but most belonged to the Llewellin family, including Tickle, a faithful friend of Lord Llewellin. Pupkin and Kitty rest there, and Nell the woodman's dog who followed him everywhere.

Upwey 🌿

One of the 'characters' of Weymouth between the two Great Wars was 'Surgeram' Shorey, a burly man with the red cheeked countenance of a Dickens villain, who sold logs from a horse and cart in winter, drove a horse bus for visitors in summer and swore heartily all the year round. His horse bus plied from the King's Statue, and for a few shillings conveyed the visitors to Upwey Wishing Well, with a cream tea thrown in. It is the place where the river Wey rises and its rare wishing well was watched over by elderly ladies who in return for money, offered a glass of the water as it bubbled from the earth in the shadow of chestnut trees. Drink and your wish will come true they predicted.

The coach and the strawberry teas are luxuries of the past and when I came to renew my aquaintance with the well and make a few more wishes I found it closed. Entrance to this magic spot is via a restaurant which is shut in the winter.

George III was luckier when in the days of Sir Christopher Wren's representation of Upwey as Member of Parliament, he came to the well and drank from a Gold Cup, which later became the original Ascot Gold Cup.

There was early confusion as to whether Upwey should be spelled Upway, in the Liberty of Wayhouse, a contraction of Wayboyeux, the property having been originally owned by the Barons Bayeux.

The church is 15th century and very beautiful, You pass it as you ascend the long winding hill to the Ridgeway, with it commanding views of Portland. It was from this spot that Thomas Hardy wrote the opening scene of his greatest work, *The Dynasts*.

Walford 🌿

The tiny hamlet of Walford, with an inn and a mill is on the outskirts of Wimborne and is rapidly being surrounded by new estates as Wimborne's population grows.

Saxons crossing the shallow river Allen at this point, having taken a tumble into the water on the stepping stones, may have commented on the dangerous state of the ford. They might have used the word *wealt*, which meant shaky or unsteady, and perhaps may have been the origin of the place name! In Domesday Book the place is recorded as Walteford.

A medieval packhorse bridge of seven arches, remodelled in 1802, has replaced the ford and speeds traffic on to Cranborne, and Walford is no longer a difficult place to cross.

Warmwell 🐝

Warmwell borrowed some of Hardy's Heath during the last war to become a forward aerodrome for fighter aircraft, thus conserving fuel for squadrons flying into battles over the Channel.

The Warmwell crossroads, now an island sorting out the Wareham traffic bound for Dorchester or Weymouth, was one of the worst accident black spots in the county in the early days of motoring. The village, hiding in a dip, is unpretentious with a 700 year old church containing a font in which Norman children were baptised.

The records of Warmwell chronicle that John Sadler, who lived in the fine 17th century Manor House, prophesied on his deathbed before witnesses, of 'dark days coming on'.

He spoke of a plague in London, a great fire, and three ships landing in the west which would cause uproar.

All these things came true, the Great Plague, followed by the Fire of London and three ships which landed with Monmouth at Lyme Regis.

The village gets its name from a well of tepid water and has a churchyard which is almost a monument to war, being filled with tombstones of German and Italian prisoners of war who worked here, and RAF fighter pilots who took off from the airfield, never to return. All are remembered.

Westbourne 🐝

In the 1870s Westbourne was described as a hamlet built around Seamoor Road, an important position on the old Bournemouth – Poole boundary.

The County Gates here not only marked the boundary between Poole and Bournemouth but also the entrance to Branksome estate. A picture taken at the turn of the century shows a little bus waiting to make a trip to Sandbanks; also in the picture are three women standing on the other side of the road exchanging gossip.

The site of this picture is very different today, because this is one of the busiest traffic junctions of the area, a meeting place of west-bound cars and those from Poole, Swanage and Sandbanks.

Westbourne will be remembered by tens of thousands of holiday-makers who started their holiday at West Station Terminus. During the August peak period over a dozen packed trains would arrive each weekend, those travellers arriving during the night and early morning thronging the Pleasure Gardens waiting for their holiday accommodation to become available at midday. Unfortunately the station was destroyed in 1965.

Florence Nightingale had an interest in Westbourne when in 1867 she was a prime mover in the building of the Herbert Home Hospital, but the area's most famous resident was none other than Robert Louis Stevenson who lived at 'Skerryvore' on the West Cliff between 1885–1887. While at this rather ordinary house he wrote *Kidnapped* and *The Strange Case of Dr. Jekyll and Mr. Hyde.*.

The name of his house comes from the lighthouse built by Stevenson's father-in-law's firm off the west coast of Argyll.

Sadly the house was badly damaged by enemy bombing during the Second World War and was later demolished to its foundations, which then formed the centre of a memorial garden to the author. In the grounds is a model of the famous lighthouse.

West Knighton

Off the Broadmayne road near Whitcombe there is a turning to West Knighton. A little place consisting of a few cottages, a church and it once had a school.

It is mentioned in the Domesday Book and in 1304 belonged to the Knights Hospitallers.

Nearby at Little Mayne is an ancient stone circle known as the Sarsen Stones, which local legend inaccurately claims to be a Druid Temple.

The 17th century farmhouse once belonged to Elizabeth Warde who died in 1635 and it later became the property of a London merchant.

West Stafford 🌾

Thomas Hardy knew West Stafford as a boy. It was only a mile or so from his birthplace at Bockhampton and he called it Talbothayes in his novels. In the story of Tess it was from Talbothayes church that the bells rang for her wedding. It is a pretty place off the beaten track.

The church has had countless restorations but it is mainly mid 1600s.

The Rev Reginald Southwell Smith lies in a tomb near the altar, probably because of his long stay as rector. He came to West Stafford the year before Queen Victoria came to the throne and he officiated there for sixty years.

An antique carving from Innsbruck, portraying Jesus being taught to read by Joseph was given to the church in 1918.

The old Rectory has a strange Jacobean fireplace in its hall and a treasured desk at which Wordsworth sat to write.

The Wise Man Inn is the name of the pub, but I can find no reason for its strange name.

Not far away is Woodsford Castle, built in 1337 and now used as a farmhouse. Its walls are 5 to 6 feet thick and it is claimed to be one of the oldest inhabited places in Dorset.

Whitchurch Canonicorum 🌾

The man who inspired Shakespeare to write *The Tempest* lies in the beautiful village of Whitchurch Canonicorum, one of the gems of the Marshwood Vale, and its 'capital'.

Sir George Somers was a man of great energy. He not only sailed with Raleigh, captured treasure ships, was Mayor of Lyme Regis where he was born, but also found time to become a Member of Parliament. He is best known for his part in the colonisation of Virginia, sailing with nine ships loaded with settlers. The fleet got scattered and his vessel wrecked on a coral island. It was one of the Bermuda Islands, the Bermoothes of Shakespeare's play.

He took possession and spent the next year rebuilding boats to eventually land his settlers in Virginia. Sadly, on a voyage back to Bermuda for more supplies, he died in 1610. His heart is buried there but they brought his body home to Whitchurch, although it would have been easier the other way round. So the place which is Bermuda on the map was known as Somers Island to his men, and Prospero's Island in Shakespeare.

The very ancient church of Whitchurch Canonicorum remembers men of many wars including a VC, Lt. Edgar Cookson, killed by the Turks at Kut-el-Amara during the 1914-18 War, and the edifice is unique in being the only parish church in England containing the bones of its patron saint. The shrine of St. Wite or Wita is in the north transept.

The appellation is anything but obvious. The same lady is the 'St. Candida' in the white stone church's name of St. Candida and St. Cross. It has also been suggested that she was St. Blanche of Brittany or a Saxon woman killed during a Danish raid.

Her shrine, in the early English north transept of the church, contains three oval holes through which pilgrims used to thrust diseased limbs or the clothing of those too ill to come in person.

In 1900 a stone repairer went even further. Working on the inner coffin, he discovered a lead casket bearing the legend, 'Hic Requiesct Reliquie Sce Wite' (here lie the remains of St. Wite). It contained some of the bones and teeth of a small woman about forty years of age.

Whitcombe ✒

A travelling historian once said of Whitcombe, 'In all this little place is not an ugly thing.'

It is even more true today. The farmhouse and surrounding cottages, as well as buttressed barn, have all been refurbished to form a neat and peaceful complex on foundations 1,000 years old.

Adjacent, in this hollow, on the Dorchester – Broadmayne road, is the little Norman church peeping through its own coppice of well-foliaged trees.

The church has been lovingly restored in memory of Dorset's dialect poet, William Barnes, and rightfully so because, as a curate, he preached his first sermon there, and in 1885, when rector of nearby Winterborne Came, he was brought to Whitcombe to preach his last. The pulpit is as he left it that morning just before his death in 1886.

Arthur Mee tells an amusing story of Barnes' days as curate at Whitcombe. In the middle of a sermon, the clerk rushed into the church shouting 'fire!!' The church emptied and pastor and flock helped fight a blaze in a hay rick. Barnes called this clerk the Archbishop of York because he used to tell people: 'Now you got to mind I; I be the second man in the church I be.'

It is a pity that this beautifully restored rural corner with its cared for memorial church, stands where the widened road sweeps down-hill and round a bend, because it has become a speed track. But those who may have passed on a day in the summer of 1983 might have been shocked to see crinolined ladies and top-hatted gents walking into the church.

Amateur Dorset film makers were enacting the last service con-ducted by the Rev. William Barnes, portrayed by a Weymouth printer, part of a film on the poet's life in readiness for the celebra-tions connected with the centenary of his death in 1986.

Wick

A village should have a church and a pub. So said Annie Bowser who lived in Riverside Cottage on a bend of the road where Wick Ferry crosses to the Christchurch shore on the other side of the Stour.

Tiny Wick, described as the last village on the Stour, had neither, but was a hamlet of great charm, with a dairy farm and delightful little cottages built around a triangular village green. Today, holiday makers at Christchurch, and the residents of the recently built estates can enjoy the unique charm of this village.

Sixty years ago Wick Lane from Tuckton twisted through a woodland and there were glimpses of the Stour through the trees on the left. Riverside Cottage, a simple 17th century thatched house faced the approaching visitor and here was a cutting in the woods to the punt style ferry. The miniature village centre with triangular green is close at hand with cottages covered by flowering creepers decorating the walls, and gardens bursting with jungles of old English flowers. The cottages still bear their sweet sounding names; amongst them, Tranquility, Quality, and Laurel. Riverside Cottage struggles to maintain its dignity beside the Ferry, which is now power propelled. The farm beside the Stour is no longer worked, and the buildings lie derelict.

Wick's greatest character was Sam Hookey 'The Wicked Man of Wick', one of the south's most infamous smugglers.

He was born in 1725, in a lowly house which has long disappeared. Researchers believe it was near the farm. His father was a fisherman and part time smuggler, and on a trip to Guernsey he abducted a beautiful Spanish girl and brought her home. Sam was the first child of ten of this romantic union. Sam was a daring child and seeking to burrow into the centre of a burial mound at Hengistbury Head became trapped by a fall of rock. His life was saved but he became permanently crippled.

After an apprenticeship, he set up as a farrier but it is believed that his smithy was merely a cloak for his far more lucrative work as a smuggler. He took part in countless smuggling runs and was often engaged in encounters with the forces of law and order.

He was fearless and, having lost an eye in an affray, wore a leather bandage over the socket. It is said that the bandage was never renewed or cleaned in over 40 years. He was known for his smuggling along the coasts of Christchurch and Poole Bay and as far inland as Salisbury, and it was his cunning in planning that earned him fame.

His greatest coup took place in Christchurch harbour at Whitsuntide, 1764. He split his gang into two forces, the smaller force running a load of brandy tubs ashore near the mouth of the Bourne at Bournemouth. When the Riding Master and his assistants arrived to intercept, Hookey's men put up a fight before being dispersed, and the Excisemen set to work opening the barrels, only to find them full of sea water.

While this farce was being enacted, Hookey's main force, consisting of three luggers, sailed into Christchurch Harbour and landed no less than 12,033 barrels of spirits, two tons of tea, and five bales of silk. It was put ashore on what was in those days a marshland, but is now the site of the Wick Ferry Holiday Camp. The people of Christchurch were well trained in hiding such cargoes and before the Excisemen returned all the contraband was safely hidden, and some already on its way to inland destinations. It was considered to be the largest single landing ever accomplished, and not a shot was fired.

158

Hookey must have enjoyed his life, spending as he 'earned' and at the age of 71 years died in a manner which was in keeping with his life style and within a few yards of home.

On a night in August 1796, he was attempting to run a cargo of tea and gold across a ford in the Stour. The party was surprised by Excisemen and in the confusion, Sam Hookey in panic stepped into a hole in the river bed, and weighed down by the gold in his pockets was drowned.

Some people say his ghost is sometimes seen thrashing the waters of the Stour at this point, which makes an interesting story for holiday-makers returning home from the holiday camp to tell their friends.

Wimborne St. Giles

This is the home of one of our noblest families, the Shaftesburys.

The 16th century house is in a vast park through which the river Allen flows, feeding a seven acre lake as it winds its way towards Wimborne. the quaintest of village signs pictures St. Giles with his hind. Wimborne St. Giles, which bears itself with dignity, is another of those sequestered places where you find yourself whispering lest you annoy the spirits of Ashleys, long dead.

Treves described the village stocks as being in a state of 'extreme senility' in 1907. Today they are scarcely recognisable, and certainly in no condition to contain the local bad boys. But the ruins have been pampered with a little well-like canopy above their rotting remains.

The first Earl, Anthony Ashley-Cooper, built the house in the 1650s in the style of Inigo Jones. During the Civil Wars, he at first sided with the King but believed in the right of Parliament to rule and, at the Coronation of Charles II, he was made a Peer and Chancellor to the Exchequer. His independent thinking was his downfall and, when holding the office of Lord Chancellor was dismissed. Later the King needed his aid and tried to bribe him, offering him a dukedom. He declined and became a leader in the Protestant cause, but when he proposed the Duke of Monmouth as a future king, he had gone too far and was thrown into the Tower and tried for high treason. He escaped to Holland where he died in 1683. A man incorruptible and faithful to his beliefs, he died a failure.

The seventh Earl lives on in the heart of the people because of his hatred of wrong and injustice. He fought the cause of Jews and Poles, and passed legislation to stop much of the child labour in the early 1800s. Journeying into home, factory and mine, he saw for himself the conditions women and children worked and lived in. He faced opposition from mine owners who were using the sweated labour of children of 5 years of age in the pits, and made Parliament aware of the plight of the poor. In one Act, chimney sweeping by boys was abolished. The seventh Earl was one of the great Parliamentarians of the Victorian era.

Wimborne St. Giles was the scene of another story concerning children. Soon after the last war the village school conducted an interesting experiment in education.

The headmaster and his teacher wife, accepting that the young village children would turn to the land for their livelihoods, ran the school as a farm. Nearby they kept pigs and sheep and a kitchen garden, which the boys ran under supervision. The girls spun the wool, dyed it and made garments from their own patterns. The running of the farm and its financial problems formed the basis of mathematics, and an official Young Farmers Club gave the children the chance to express themselves publicly. Alas, educational practices have changed the age group attending the school, and the idea has long been forgotten.

Winfrith Newburgh

No village could be more Dorset than Winfrith Newburgh, with its long lonely street of thatched cottages which look as if they have not been disturbed since the last century, except those ripped out like rotten teeth to be replaced by modern houses. Sheltered under the high Downs, it lies on the road to Lulworth Cove, with the church standing at one end above a stream and surrounded by well-used farm buildings.

The other Winfrith, a mile away, belongs to another world because an atomic energy station has grown up there. A concrete jungle of strange shapes resembling a colony of invaders from outer space who have set up camp on the heather of Hardy's sacred heath.

When the development was first announced in the 1960s there was a public outcry and I visited the Blasted Heath to record its lonely beauty. The winter wind whistled through the dead russet-coloured fern, and suddenly I was surprised by two Ghurka soldiers, armed and camouflaged with fern tucked under their helmets. They looked far less colourful than the soldiers of Hardy's Dynasts, and they mumbled a greeting and moved away on their manoeuvre. Two years later, Atomic Winfrith dominated the lonely Heath.

Between the new and old Winfriths, within view of the main road, is a home of rare beauty. Spicers Cottage is a blaze of colour in summer with hydrangeas, marigolds and roses around lush green lawns.

The old church which was restored in 1852 has a beam supporting the chancel dated 1220.

Winterborne Came 🐦

On my journeys the name of Parson Barnes, rector, poet and student of the English lanugage, has been mentioned countless times and it was as rector of Winterborne Came that he ended his days. In 1886, William Barnes at the age of 86 died peacefully in his sleep in the thatched rectory off the main Dorchester – Broadmayne road. It is still a residence, caressed in neat thatch and cared for, with a beautiful garden.

My last visit to the rectory was made in the fading light of a spring evening. The yellowing sun warmed the walls of the cottages, the thick thatch casting a faint shadow on the pink washed walls. In the little wood, which shields it from the main road, dying daffodils drooped in the shadows.

A mile away, the little 13th century church with a panelled Jacobean pulpit keeps company with the 18th century Came House in a small wood. There is no more peaceful park in Dorset, and Barnes lies in a simple grave beneath the church wall. Strange that this man of peace should be sharing his last resting place with two warriors of war.

Inside the church are memorials to Col. Dawson-Damor, who had two horses shot from beneath him at Waterloo, and there is a wooden cross from the grave of his kinsman, Seymour Dawson-Damor, who fell in the 1914-18 War.

Winterborne Clenston
& Anderson

There are 14 Winterborne villages in Dorset on the banks of two rivulets rising in chalk hills, and Anderson and Clenston boast ancient manor houses.

The house at Anderson is a stately building, brick-faced with stone, high gables and towering chimneys. Features are the stone mullioned windows. There is little else at Anderson and the church topped with two school style bells in an open tower is now a private chapel, with a little gate leading into the gardens of the big house. The stream is bridged and protected by a balustrade of short tubby pillars. I could imagine crinolined ladies strolling to church between flower lined paths long ago, but my visit was in dour December and it all looked very sad.

Above Clenston, on the Downs, is Comb's Ditch, an earthwork and relic of the once great line of defence.

Winterborne Houghton

Thomas Hardy is responsible for the people of Winterborne Houghton being called 'Houghton Owls'. His rustic joke in *Far from the Madding Crowd* concerned bashful Joseph Poorgrass, who lost his way at night in Yalbury Wood, having had too much to drink. In fear at being lost he cried out 'Man-a-lost, man-a-lost'. At the same time a passing owl happened to be calling 'Whoo-whoo-whoo', and Joseph, now thoroughly scared, replied 'Joseph Poorgrass of Weatherby Sir'.

Although admitting the story against himself he tried to save face by denying he called the bird 'Sir'.

'What's right is right' he said, 'I never said sir to the bird, knowing very well that no man of gentleman's rank would be hollering there at that time of night.'

This is where the most western of the two Dorset Winterbornes rises to continue through eight villages bearing its name before it meets the river Stour.

The church of St. Andrew is in flint and dated 1862.
On Meriden Down, one mile WNW of the village is a Romano-British settlement, surrounded by a 'celtic' field system.

Winterborne Kingston

If the Romans who built the Icknield Way through what is now known as Winterborne Kingston had returned in the early 1980s they would have thought the place infested with Pterodactyls. A flying school used adjacent fields to this ancient highway to teach micro-flying. On closer inspection they would have been more frightened to see that the 'birds' carried men. Now flying has ceased there and the village is at peace again.

Hut circles are traced on higher ground – remains of an ancient British village. It is believed that a king was buried here in a gold coffin and when a lead box was dug up by a ploughman in the last century, there was great excitement. But there was no gold coffin inside, only the remains of a young Roman in nail studded sandals. A man who walked this way 1500 years ago who dissolved quickly into dust.

Winterborne Muston

The guide books seem to have forgotten this village, but it can be found on the Ordnance Survey map, where it is shown as a farm and a handful of buildings between Winterborne Kingston and Anderson. However, connoisseurs of architecture would be well rewarded by venturing down the cul-de-sac to inspect the 17th century thatched cottage, extended on each side during the 18th century, when it also had a polygonal porch added.

The Exchequer records of the year 1195 in Richard I's reign show that this place was held by a member of the de Mustiers who came from Moutiers in France. Muston was known as Winterborn Musters 700 years ago.

WINTERBORNE TOMSON. — JOHN BAKER

Winterborne Tomson 🐚

Winterborne Tomson can easily be missed because the way into this hamlet is little more than a farmgate, but it is the most interesting of the Blandford Winterbornes.

The tiny 15th century church with a curvacious apsidal east end and a squat wooden tower, stands in a farmyard. A horse whinnied as I walked across the churchyard with its single tomb, and aroused two others who came to their stable doors to watch me.

For many years the church was deserted. Pulpit dusty, curtains and altar cloth motheaten and in shreds – until some autographed documents on architecture by Thomas Hardy were sold to provide funds for the repair of this pathetic ruin. It was restored in 1932 as a memorial to the author.

A notice states that 'St. Andrews was restored by the Redundant Churches Fund of St. Andrew by the Wardrobe, London.'

Winterborne Whitchurch 🐚

The motorist may hardly notice Winterborne Whitchurch if he is hurrying from Salisbury to Dorchester, but this little village was the birthplace of John Wesley's father and if that sounds too much like distant name dropping, I can also tell you that this place on the banks of the Winterborne was also the birthplace of Elizabethan George Turberville. Now, before you say 'who's he?', let me hasten

164

to add that he was not only a scholar of Winchester College, at the age of 14 years, but went to the Empress of Russia's Court as secretary to Ambassador Thomas Randolph.

Yet this brilliant scholar and poet, who described the Russians as 'a people passing rude to vices vile inclined,' and wrote volumes on hunting, falconry, as well as sonnets and songs, is forgotten and so are his works.

The 15th century church has a unique pulpit, brought here from the old church demolished at Milton Abbas when Joseph Damer destroyed a whole village.

It appears that the pulpit from the old Milton Abbas church was not considered good enough for the new edifice, and when a fire seriously damaged Winterborne Whitchurch church in 1867, they borrowed the discarded pulpit. It had been plastered over and tarred to save it from rotting as it lay in a yard at Milton Abbey. A Rev. Wynne had it sent to London where experts restored it and added the figures of the four Apostles. I hope my story does not remind the authorities at Milton Abbas and cause them to ask for it back.

Winterborne Zelstone 🌿

This surely must be Dorset's prettiest and most peaceful village. Off the main Wimborne to Dorchester road, it descends to the valley, past thatched cottages dressed in pastel pink, with pale blue windows.

Ducks were standing around the shrunken village pond disgusted because although it was November, the pond was almost dry and the Winterborne itself had just enough water to soak the rotting russet leaves on its shallow bed. Over a little bridge the path to the church takes you beside more thatched cottages with walls in virgin white.

The church has no ornate memorials to sons long dead, but a solitary wooden plaque dated 1957 tells that the lighting was given in memory of the Barrett family, and of the unknown benefactor who gave a field long ago for the maintenance of this church.

A notice board bore an amusing coloured cartoon of bellringers and press cuttings telling how the Royal Corps of Signals gave the organ to St. Marys and kept it in repair.

A medieval stone cross stands on the river bank, re-erected to commemorate the Silver Jubilee of Queen Elizabeth II in 1977.

165

Winterbourne Abbas ✿

Whenever there was a drought during my early days as a news photographer, I came to the Winterbourne village and photographed children playing football in the dried out river bed, using the quaint little bridges which link the cottages to the road as goal posts. Worried looking mothers stood by with empty pails.

Of course it was cheating a little, because the Winterborne, as its name suggests, only flows in the winter months. Winterbourne Abbas is one of the villages in this shallow valley.

Situated just south of Dorchester, it is natural to find barrows and burial mounds and it is thought that the Romans had a large camp here. Along the main road and fenced off are 'The Nine Stones'. These are set in a circle and were probably a place of worship.

The Church of St. Mary with its 15th century tower is reached by crossing a little bridge. The fact that the church was one of the last in the country to have a band is commemorated by a memorial and an instrument which hangs on the wall. The nave has a gallery which projects over nearly half of it, and there is a crooked chancel.

With the Dissolution of the Monasteries the living was granted to Howard, Viscount Bindon, and eventually to Lincoln College, Oxford. Although there has been a church at Winterbourne Abbas since Saxon times, nothing of that original building remains except the base of the south wall. In 1894 the church was re-roofed with timber from New Zealand. One of the peal of bells bears the impress of a Plantagenet coin.

Reference was made earlier to the church band. Modern church-goers seem to know little about this musical practice which was popular from the end of the 18th century till the end of the 19th. The Rev. John Bryant in the 1982 Dorset Year Book, gives some interesting facts about the custom and particularly the Winterbourne Abbas band.

Although the last Dorset band did not disappear until 1895, the Winterbourne group played their last notes in 1881. Organs, apparently had gone out of fashion, the villagers preferring the home spun music. The author referred to a three piece band. The thatcher played the clarinet and acted as leader, a farm labourer was the flautist and the bass was in the hands of the shepherd. There was no violin because the parson said it 'savoured of the public house'. The band played at the west end of the church on a rising platform, the violin, cello and flute playing at a long desk on the lower steps, while the clarinet stood a step above flanked by the singers.

The most famous band in the valley was that of Winterbourne St. Martin. At one time the group consisted of four clarinets, a hautboy and a 'base-viol'. The hautboy player was a mason who also blew the loud bassoon in the village band.

It is said that there is nothing new under the sun so perhaps we should not register surprise when pop groups strum their instruments in church today to the annoyance of traditionalists.

Witchampton

The clustered centre of Witchampton, with Manor House, ruin of the manorial barn, and a long derelict water mill, – all overlooked by the church – could well be called the front garden of Dorset. The lovely thatched cottages, some with timber-framed walls, are cloaked with roses, jasmine and honeysuckle in summer, and gar-

167

dens compete to give the best showing of the old fashioned flowers of the country.

A church style door, studded and pointed at the top, leads into the village post office and store, from which emits constant chatter and happy laughter as villagers meet and exchange gossip. The church lych-gate stands next to an elegant War Memorial raised to the sons of Witchampton and Crichel, who gave their lives in conflict, and circular mounting block stands amongst the tombstones near the church door. Until very recent years, the church had a unique system whereby the visitor could put a few pence into a slot and have a choice of hearing a recording of the bells, the Hallelujah Chorus, or a short sermon from the vicar. It is no long in operation and a notice announces that the church now raises funds by means of bingo.

Even in January, Witchampton – whose old mill was once turned by the little river Allen – still has a flower show. Snowdrops wave on the banks of the church dedicated to St. Mary, St. Cuthberga and All Saints, but the motorist negotiating the tricky twists in the road, seldom sees them.

Woodcutts

'The cottages in the woods' is the derivation of the name Woodcutts, and variations such as Woodcote and Woodcott denote numerous Saxon settlements. The pleasant little hamlet of Woodcutts on the northern borders of Dorset with its homes built round a neat commonland bears no resemblance to the ancient village close at hand. This was inhabited by men who lived there from the Iron Age through the Roman period until the site's abandonment about 370 AD.

A high Downland settlement, it was first occupied just prior to the Roman conquest as a single farmstead. Throughout its habitation, the peasant farmers continued to live in a succession of wooden huts, with little except the style of pottery to distinguish their Romano-British way of life from that of their Iron Age ancestors.

Woodcutts fascinated the early archaeologist General Pitt-Rivers, who excavated the settlement at the end of the 19th century, collected valuable artifacts and skeletons, and obtained

168

enough knowledge to enable him to build fascinating models of the village and its way of life.

When the General had finished his excavations, like all good archaeologists he neatly replaced the turf, but you can still wander through the gorselands of this ancient place in the heart of the Cranborne Chase, and with more interest if you have seen the models made of the village which are now housed in Salisbury Museum, since Farnham Museum was sold up.

Woodyates 🌿

It is believed that 2,000 years ago a British city stood on a north Dorset hillside where there was a pass between the Downs of Cranborne Chase, but the village of Woodyates, which exists now, bears little resemblance to the city situated on the Icknield Way which once boasted a famous coaching inn.

Today it is an insignificant hamlet with nothing left of its historic past, unless I mention that Robert Browning's grandfather, a clerk to the Bank of England, lived here and according to historian, Arthur Mee, the old man was more concerned that the young poet should not stand on his gouty foot than hearing his early poetry.

What is left of Woodyates stands in Dorset's Khyber Pass, a way through the wooded hills of Cranborne Chase, the way from London to Weymouth. A pass that has been a stronghold since man first lived here.

Wdegeate, from the Old English wudige geat, the wooded gate has seen much fighting as well as the making of history.

To the famous old inn came Monmouth in 1685 to enact another of those historical and amusing chases which seem famous in Dorset. It was there that the Duke, fleeing from Sedgemoor and hoping to get to the coast at Poole, split up with his companion Lord Grey. They left their horses and proceeded across country singly and in disguise. Monmouth in the clothes of a shepherd was soon discovered under a hedge at Horton and both he and Grey were beheaded in London a few days later.

Wool & Bovington

Hardy's Great Heath encompasses Wool, bleak Gallows Hill and the old Abbey of Bindon, but generations of soldiers who have served in the Royal Tank Corps will remember an oil-lit station and the porter's cry of 'Wool, Wool, change for Lulworth and Bovington'. The home base of Tankmen is close at hand.

The part of Wool seen by the traveller leading east or west is modern and scattered, all except the magnificent 17th century gabled Manor House beside a bridge two centuries older, with recesses for walkers, which crosses the river Frome. The scene, framed through the tall grasses, with resident swans rummaging around in the massive cutwaters, is a must for every visiting camera enthusiast.

Wool suffers from Hardy's brilliant writing. The Manor, the old seat of the Turbervilles, is popularly accepted as the place where fictional Tess spent her honeymoon night. To confuse still further, Bindon Abbey – or all that remains of this centre founded for the Cistercians in 1172 – still has the empty open coffin of Abbot Richard de Maners on site, and it was to here that fictional, sleepwalking Angel Clare carried Tess in Hardy's novel. The author's story seems more real than historical fact.

The last abbot surrendered to the king in 1539 and in 1664 the larger part of the Abbey was burned down. Much of the stone went into the building of Lulworth Castle.

Gallows Hill, on the sombre, windswept heath, not only provides a viewpoint but has a permanent grandstand, from which visiting military personnel from all over the world watch the developing power of our armoured forces.

Lawrence of Arabia's cottage at Clouds Hill is near and it was on one of the lonely roads of this heath that he met his death in a motorcycle accident in 1935.

The famous Tank Museum contains vehicles from many nations. At an amusing, yet dignified, ceremony a few years ago, a party of German officers came bearing two crates of champagne with the request 'Could we have one of our tanks back ?' The museum authorities, who had two of the particular type, obliged.

The Museum proudly owns the Union Jack which flew over Tobruk throughout the siege in the Desert Campaign of the

Second World War, but has loaned one of its most treasured possessions to Lincoln. One of the first tanks of the Great War, 'The Flirt', which stood guarding the main gate of the Tank Museum for 30 years, has gone back to the city where it was built.

Woolland

The meadows of a rich chalkland beneath Bulbarrow Hill can have changed little since the Saxons lived there.

One such hutted settlement was Woolland, but they called it Wonland, meadowland (Old English Wynn-Land).

Although Woolland was old a thousand years ago, there is little left of the ancient place today.

Gilbert Scott designed the new church with its tower pinpointing the village in 1855. From the older church, however, was saved a font bowl of 15th century origin. The mock Gothic Manor nearby is not much older. Superb views repay the visitor who climbs to the hilltop, a patchwork of yellow and green divided by thick hedges and small woods. The view beyond Blackmore Vale goes deep into Somerset.

So it was that the Saxons, who reflected local scenery in their place names, built their huts beneath Bulbarrow and named their settlement after the meadowland.

Worbarrow

One of the most beautiful bays in Dorset, yet because it comes within the Lulworth Range area is only open to the public on rare holiday occasions. This sweeping pebble beach backed by cliffs of white has Worbarrow Tout at one end, a hill of marble and gypsum. Beneath it is Pondfield Cove. There is a mile of beach to be enjoyed and beyond, but out of bounds at all times, Flowers Barrow, a great cliff over 550 feet high.

Where you reach the bay from Tyneham, there used to be a few quaint fishermen's cottages with drooping stone roofs and just before the Second World War a new bungalow was erected styled like the cottages. Scarcely had it been lived in than the War Lords took over the village. Today like the older cottages it lies in ruins.

Worth Matravers

When Farmer Jesty appeared before the doctors of the London Vaccine Pock Institution in the year of Trafalgar, he became the most famous son of Worth Matravers.

Benjamin and his wife now lie in the graveyard of the beautiful church on a Purbeck hillside commanding views of the English Channel. The inscription on their stone reads 'An upright and honest man, particularly noted for having been the first person (known) that introduced the Cow Pox by inoculation, and who from his great strength of mind, made the experiment from the cow on his wife and two sons in the year 1774'.

You might think that the strength of mind required by his family is also worth some recognition. Farmer Jesty had noticed that dairymaids and cowmen seldom suffered from smallpox but had usually had cowpox, a milder complaint. So before Jenner had started his experiments, the Dorset farmer, aided by a knitting needle, inoculated his family with cowpox. So impressed were the London doctors that they had his portrait painted as a token of their respect.

The church, one of the oldest in Dorset, and the cottages grouped around a small duckpond is built of stone hewn from Worth's field. The whole area is honeycombed by centuries of quarrying. A Saxon doorway is blocked up in the 12th century church walls and the Norman tower stands proud in spite of a modern roof.

Higher up the village slope is a cosy inn called the Square and Compass, but its whitewashed exterior makes it look more like an inn from the Devon coast.

Wyke

Exocet, Sam, Cruise and Polaris are the fearsome weapons of modern war, but how many remember that the most lethal weapon of the two Great Wars was the torpedo, made at Wyke Regis.

The Whitehead torpedos were tested inside Portland Harbour. Launched from the breakwater at Bincleaves minus warheads they passed under a series of platforms from which men waved a red flag to signify the weapon's passage. An amusing form of communication by modern standards, yet only about 60 years ago. A second firing station launched the underwater weapon across the Weymouth Bay and, of course, there were countless stories of errant torpedos going astray, chasing boats, and one gave itself up on the beach at Castle Cove.

Mainly, Wyke is a vast dormitory for Weymouth spreading its houses around the main road from Weymouth to Portland, but old Wyke lies in a little valley at the highest point of the village. The magnificent church, once the mother church of Weymouth, has the only peal of bells in the area. On a clear summer's night, the eight bells can be heard at the seaside resort, the chimes wafting down the hillside.

The three graveyards surrounding it are of interest to those who make a hobby of tombstone spotting, because the proximity of the Channel seas of Dead Man's Bay has resulted in many mass drownings. The disastrous storm of November 18 1795 wrecked the troop transports *Venus*, *Piedmont*, and *Catherine*, and over 200 soldiers were buried along the Chesil Beach and 27 interred in one of the churchyards. In a single grave lie 140 passengers and crew of the East Indiaman *Alexander* wrecked in 1815, and 80 of the 300 lost when the *Earl of Abergavenny*, captained by the brother of poet Wordsworth, foundered in the Shambles shoal in 1805, rest in peace at Wyke.

The north side of the church of All Saints, closely associated with shipwreck and smugglers, was at one time known as the 'Devils Side', the burial place of criminals and suicides.

The figurehead corbals above the pillars have unique carvings including a stone mason, a man with a hod, and a dog with a bone in its mouth, and a painted coat of arms of George I, in the northwest wall later had two more number ones added to change it to George III; an early act of economy.

Wynford Eagle 🦅

An amusing story is told of a 'fiddle' by a member of the Sydenham family who lived on the estate at Wynford Eagle, near Maiden Newton from 1551 to 1709.

It was an inglorious end to the reign of an illustrious family. William Sydenham offered the estate as a lottery prize arranging for the winning ticket to come to a woman friend, who was to return the estate to William for a reward. However, the woman refused to give up her prize and William refused to leave the house. He ended in Dorchester Prison and died there nine years later.

It was Thomas Sydenham, one of five sons of the senior Sydenham who during the Civil Wars brought fame to the family. Thomas quit Oxford and with his brothers joined the Commonwealth Army. Always in the thick of battle, Thomas was once left on the battlefield as dead.

When he returned to civilian life, he resumed his studies at Oxford, took a medical degree and set up a practice in London.

He became known as the Father of Medicine, ignoring the concoctions produced as medicine with ingredients often harmful to the patient, and used his learning to discover new treatments. He was the first to use tincture of opium, and introduced quinine as a cure for the plague. When other doctors fled from the disease he stayed with his patients in London during the Great Plague and came through unscathed.

Jealous colleagues minimised his successes and it was many years after his death that his work gained full recognition in this country, although Continental schools recognised him for all his skills in medicine. Oddly enough he could not cure his own gout from which he suffered from early manhood.

Yetminster

If you are a confirmed loyalist, Yetminster is the place in which to take up residence. Six times a day the bells of the Minster of St. Andrew chime out the National Anthem.

The bells belong to a faceless clock, 300 years old, but it was to celebrate Queen Victoria's Jubilee that the chimes were installed.

If you are imagining the population of this lovely village, built of stone, all standing to attention when the bells chime out, then you will be disappointed. Pints were being served when I called in the local inn and happy laughter continued as the bells sounded, and when I asked a friendly native why he was not standing to attention, I received a short but friendly reply which I choose not to print here.

However, the act of keeping the chimes going is a labour of love for a team of village men. Every day one of them has to climb the 50 odd steps in the belfry to wind up the three movements.

Recently the residents, to enhance their beautiful village spent £8,000 in an effort to remove unsightly overhead electric cables.

Background Reading

For fifty years, Sir Frederick Treves (*Highways & Byways of Dorset*) and Arthur Mee (*The Kings England, Dorset*) have been constant companions on my rural journeys. I would have enjoyed the company of Sir Frederick on my present pilgrimage and to have heard his dry humour as he surveyed Dorset of the 1980s.

I must thank Southern Newspapers PLC for allowing me to browse in their extensive libraries at Bournemouth and Weymouth, and librarians Kate Brennan and Michaela Horsfield (Bournemouth), and Denise Smith (Weymouth) who were tolerant of my many requests.

Dovecote Press, *A Dorset Camera 1914-45*, refreshed my memory of events almost forgotten, and Barrie & Jenkins *The Piddle Valley Cookbook* gave me amusing food for thought.

Southern Newspaper's *What's In A Name* written by my late colleague R.K. Palmer, and illustrated by myself, my own Southern Newspaper publication *In the Steps Of William Barnes* and a rare edition of Barnes's *Poems Of Rural Life in the Dorset Dialect*, published in 1905 by Kegan Paul, Trench, Trubner & Co. – all feature in my narrative.

Aubrey de Selincourt's *The Channel Shore* and John Grimson's *The Channel Coasts of England* published by Robert Hale, made interesting reading from a nautical angle. Also *Smuggling In Hampshire & Dorset* by Geoffrey Morley (Countryside Books)

Parnham House, Beaminster

Index

Some Interesting Dorset Folk

St Aldhelm
First Bishop of Sherborne in AD 705. Patron Saint of Dorset. Headland on Dorset coast named after him.

King Alfred
Thought to have been proclaimed King at Wimborne. He scattered the Danish fleet off Swanage.

Mary Anning
Known as 'the Fossil Woman of Lyme Regis'. Discovered the first remains of a Pterodactyl in the cliffs in 1828.

Jane Austen
Famous novelist, lived at Lyme Regis which is mentioned in her novel *Persuasion*.

Baden-Powell
Founder of the Boy Scout movement. A Major General in the Boer War he established the first camp for Boy Scouts on Brownsea Island in Poole Harbour in 1907.

Sir John Bankes
Founder of the famous Dorset family and owner of Corfe Castle. A close associate of King Charles I in the 17th century.

Lady Mary Bankes
Wife of Sir John. Well known for leading the defence of Corfe Castle in 1646 in the absence of Sir John serving the King at Oxford.

William Barnes
Dorset dialect poet. Born in 1800 at Bagber Heath, the schoolmaster turned rector published *Poems of Rural Life*.

John and William Bastard
Blandford architects who rebuilt the town after the great fire of 1731.

J E Beale
James Edward Beale came from Weymouth to Bournemouth in 1881 to found the famous family store Beales of Bournemouth.

Dennis Bond
Member of the Whig family who lived at Creech Grange. Leading figure on the side of Parliament in the 17th century. MP for Dorchester.

Rupert Brooke
In the 19th century at Bournemouth Brooke discovered poetry after reading the works of Robert Browning. He became a famous World War I poet.

Jake Bolson
Founder of the great fleet of pleasure boats operating from Bournemouth beach. His call 'Any more for the Skylark' is known to millions of holidaymakers.

George Burt
A master builder in the 19th century, one of the founders of Swanage.

Robert Cecil, 1st Earl of Salisbury
He was a chief minister for Elizabeth I. The family has owned Cranborne for centuries.

John Churchill
As Duke of Marlborough, Churchill was a great soldier. Son of Winston Churchill of Minterne Magna. One time MP for Lyme Regis.

Sir Alan Cobham
A great aviation pioneer. Known for his 'Flying Air Circus' between Wars and founder of a flight refuelling business at Tarrant Rushton.

Joseph Damer
First Earl of Dorchester. Famous as the man who re-sited and rebuilt the village of Milton Abbas in the 18th century so that he could build a great residence next to Milton Abbey.

Charles Darwin
The author of *Origin of the Species* lived for a while in Bourne-mouth.

Daniel Defoe
Famous author who wrote glowingly of the county.

The Digby Family
Have owned Sherborne Castle since the early 1600s. A large family with countless Royal connections.

George Bubb Doddington
Wealthy Dorset squire in the 17th and 18th centuries and an eccentric who was MP for Weymouth.

John Galsworthy
The famous literary figure who died in 1933 went to school in Bournemouth.

King George III
Chose Weymouth for his holidays. In 1789 was the first King to bathe from a bathing machine.

Isaac Gulliver
Most successful of all the Dorset smugglers. Lived mainly in Kinson where he built a house with smugglers' hides.

Sir Dan Godfrey
Formed the Bournemouth Municipal Orchestra and put Bourne-mouth on the music map. He served 41 years from 1893 to 1934.

Sir Charles Groves
Eminent British conductor who, after the last war, built up the Bournemouth Symphony Orchestra.

Tony Hancock
Leading comedian in post-war years. Born in Bournemouth and educated at Swanage.

Thomas Hardy
Born 1840 at Upper Bockhampton near Dorchester, his novels won him a special place in English literature. He used the county as a background to novels like *Tess of the D'Urbervilles*.

Admiral Sir Thomas Masterman Hardy
Born in Portisham he became Captain of Nelson's *Victory*. Nelson died in his arms at the Battle of Trafalgar.

Rev John Hutchins
18th century Rector of Wareham who wrote the definitive *History of Dorset*. His detailed work provided the basis for future historians' writings.

Stuart Hibberd
Dorset-born and educated at Weymouth College, he became the BBC's first chief announcer and famous for his impeccable enunciation.

Judge Jeffreys
The infamous judge who ran the 'Bloody Assize' in Dorset after the Monmouth Rebellion in 1685. During the trial at Dorchester 74 followers of Monmouth were executed and 175 transported to the West Indies.

Benjamin Jesty
In 1774 Farmer Jesty successfully inoculated his family with Cow Pox with the aid of a darning needle to prove it would protect them from the more dreaded Smallpox.

Augustus John
Distinguished painter who lived at Poole with his large family.

Henry Lamb
The Australian-born artist loved Dorset and often worked there. He painted his much acclaimed giant painting *Advanced Dressing Station on the Struma* at Stourpaine in 1920. Locals were the models. His portrait of Sir Dan Godfrey angered the conductor and the painting was eventually banished to the cellars of Bournemouth Pavilion.

Lillie Langtry
Actress and society beauty. She was the mistress of the Prince of Wales, the future Edward VII. Her house in Bournemouth's Derby Road is now the Langtry Manor Hotel.

Lord Llewellin
John Justin Llewellin of Upton House, Poole, a country gentleman and genial host. He had a distinguished career in politics which reached a peak in 1953 when he was appointed first Governor General and Commander-in-Chief of the Federation of Rhodesia and Nyasaland.

T E Lawrence
Legendary Lawrence of Arabia helped the Arabs to gain control of their lands from the Turks during the First World War. Died in a motor-cycle accident near his cottage at Moreton in 1935. Author of *The Seven Pillars of Wisdom.*

George Loveless
Leader of the Tolpuddle Martyrs, the six men of Dorset who fought for a reasonable living wage. Because they took an oath of allegiance they were convicted and transported to a penal colony and later, through public demand, were pardoned.

Rodney Legg
Prolific writer on Dorset and its walks. Led the campaign to get the Army ranges of Tyneham open to the public after the last World War.

James, Duke of Monmouth
Eldest illegitimate son of Charles II. He landed at Lyme Regis in an attempt to seize the throne from his uncle James II. Beaten at the Battle of Sedgemoor.

John Morton
Borne at Milborne St Andrew. Became Archbishop of Canterbury in 1486.

John Mowlem
Poor Swanage boy who went to London and eventually founded the great building company of Mowlem. In retirement became a benefactor of this little seaside resort.

John Makepeace
Present owner of Parnham House near Beaminster where he designs and builds furniture. One of the world's top craftsmen, he specialises in unique offerings.

Rodney Pattisson
Poole Yachtsmen who won Olympic Gold medals in the Flying Dutchman Class.

Theodore Powys
Theodore and his brothers John Cowper and Llewelyn were Purbeck-based authors, living in cottages at White Nose and East Chaldon.

General August Pitt-Rivers
Historian who built the now extinct museum of old farming implements at Farnham. Known as the 'Father of Modern Archaeology'.

Sir Walter Raleigh
Elizabethan courtier, adventurer, soldier and writer. First owner of Sherborne Castle.

Sir Merton Russell-Cotes
A Bournemouth benefactor who owned the Royal Bath Hotel. He and Lady Cotes gave their home on the East Cliff for the town's museum. He was Mayor of the town in 1894, although he never served on the Council.

Sir Percy Florence Shelley
Only son of poet Percy Bysshe Shelley, lived at Boscombe Manor.

Mary Shelley
Second wife of the poet Shelley. As an author she created Frankenstein.

Sir George Somers
Lyme Regis man responsible for discovering Bermuda. A sailor and explorer, he was shipwrecked on one of the islands.

Robert Louis Stevenson
While living in Bournemouth he wrote *Kidnapped* and *Dr Jekyll and Mr Hyde*.

Marie Stopes
Eminent doctor who shocked Britain with her outspoken writings and books on contraception and birth control in the 1920s. After two failed marriages she died alone in her lighthouse home at Portland Bill.

Captain Lewis Tregonwell
Acclaimed as the founder of Bournemouth when he built his home in Exeter Road in 1810. He had known the area earlier when he commanded troops at Bournemouth awaiting invasion by Napoleon.

Sir James Thornhill
Dorset-born painter famous for his decorative work on the cupola, lantern and whispering gallery of St Paul's Cathedral. He died in 1721 and his best known local work is the reredos at St Mary's Church, Weymouth, depicting The Last Supper.

Sir Frederick Treves
A shy schoolboy who became a famous Dorset figure. As an eminent surgeon he served Queen Victoria and Kings Edward VII and George V. A great traveller and writer, he was author of *The Elephant Man* and *The Highways and Byways of Dorset*. He was first President of the Society of Dorset Men.

J M W Turner
The famous artist was a frequent visitor to Dorset painting sunsets over Poole Harbour.

Richard Todd
Popular British film star resided at Broadstone as a child.

Archbishop Wake
William Wake, born at Shapwick in 1657 was destined to become Archbishop of Canterbury in 1715. He became unpopular because he suggested that every child, regardless of station, should have equal opportunity to learn.

Thomas Wedgewood
A member of the pottery family. Lived at Estbury House. He conducted early experiments in photography.

Joseph Weld
In 1964 Joseph, a member of the Dorset Catholic Weld family was appointed Lord Lieutenant of the County. An ancestor, Thomas Weld, was the first English Cardinal appointed by the Pope. The ancestral home of the Welds is Lulworth Castle, destroyed by fire between the two World Wars.

John Wesley
The founder of Methodism was the grandson of another John Wesley, vicar of Winterborne Whitchurch in the 17th century. His grandfather, John, was imprisoned at Poole for his non-conformist beliefs.

Ralph Wightman
Author and broadcaster. He became nationally the voice of rural England and spoke in dialect to the World in a Christmas Day round the World link-up in the 1930s. He was born at Piddletrenthide.

Sir Mortimer Wheeler
Eminent archaeologist, excavated Maiden Castle in the 1930s.

Mary Wollstonecraft
Buried in St Peter's Churchyard, Bournemouth. 18th century exponent of Women's Rights and author of feminist literature.

Sir Christopher Wren
The famous architect served as MP for Melcombe Regis. After the Great Fire of London he rebuilt St Paul's with Portland stone.